I READ IT IN THE LOCAL RAG

Further details of Poppyland Publishing titles can be found at
www.poppyland.co.uk
*where clicking on the 'Support and Resources' button
will lead to pages specially compiled to support this book.*

I read it in the local rag

Gleanings from
Norfolk and Suffolk newspapers
1700–1900

PIP WRIGHT

POPPYLAND
PUBLISHING

ISBN 0 946148 78 3 / 978 0 946148 78 3

Published by Poppyland Publishing, Cromer NR27 9AN

Acknowledgements

are due to a number of people without whose help
the publication of this book would not have been possible.
In particular, thanks are due to the staff at the Suffolk Record Offices
at Ipswich, Bury St Edmunds and Lowestoft,
the Family History Centre at Norwich,
the museums at Cromer, Halesworth and Beccles
and the libraries at Kings Lynn, Thetford and Great Yarmouth.

Pictures in this book are taken from contemporary sources such as paintings,
sketches and cartoons, newspaper illustrations and adverts,
supported by early twentieth century postcards
and photographs taken by the author.

Extracts from the papers have been transcribed as they appear in the original,
except that obvious typographical errors have been silently corrected
and punctuation occasionally amended for clarity and ease of reading.

Designed and typeset in 11 on 14 pt Elysium by Watermark, Cromer NR27 9HL

Printed by Printing Services (Norwich) Ltd

Contents

A caricature by Bunbury of Roger Marden, the first vendor of the BURY POST

Introduction

On October 24th 1730, the IPSWICH JOURNAL published this story:

Last Wednesday night, an unfortunate accident happened to a servant at Mr. Edgar's of Sproughton near this town; as she was sitting under a cart lodge milking a cow, part of the said cart lodge fell on her and bruised her to that degree that she died within a few minutes. 'Twas remarkable that the cow, at the fall of the lodge, sprung out and was saved.

What does this short story tell us about the people living in East

Anglia nearly three hundred years ago? Well, in the opinion of the writer, the cow seems to have been more important than the poor milkmaid. Though we are told who the owner of the farm was, the girl's name is a mystery. But then, the readers of this early local paper would have been land-owners and businessmen. They were the only ones likely to be able to afford a newspaper, and the only ones likely to be able to read it.

At this time, sea-captains were still trading in slaves, criminals were publicly whipped or branded for petty theft, and small boys were still being sent up chimneys.

By our standards today, it seems to have been a cruel age, and this can be seen in many of the stories that appeared in these early local papers. Of course, the language is a bit strange; they wrote using long sentences, full of long words, but the humour and the fun still comes through.

One Elizabeth Farry of Lanark in Scotland was proclaimed (in order to marriage) on Sunday, was married on Monday, had a child on Tuesday, her husband stole a horse on Wednesday, for which he was banished on Thursday, the child died on Friday, and was buried on Saturday, all in one week.

IPSWICH GAZETTE February 7th 1736

Now which nursery rhyme does that remind you of?

Of course, just because it appeared in the paper did not mean you had to believe every word, any more than you do when reading papers today, but it is amazing what you can learn about our ancestors from the news that was published at the time.

Three hundred years ago, people heard the news by word of mouth. Local carriers and stage-coach drivers swopped stories with the people they met in the coaching inns and beer-houses along the roads and tracks they travelled. By the time these stories had been retold a few dozen times, they probably became rather exaggerated, but people really wanted to know what was going on outside their own town or village.

As early as 1620, small pamphlets were being published, telling of disasters around the kingdom - the 'Wofull newes' of fires, floods

and famine. But these were only occasional publications. Soon, newspapers printed in London were being carried aboard every stage-coach to all parts of the country. Seventeenth-century news-

A woodcut picture from a pamphlet reporting a flood in Monmouth in 1607

papers like the LONDON GAZETTE reported on all the great events of the day from the Great Fire of London to the crowning of King William of Orange.

Then, in the late 1690s, in several parts of the country, the first local weekly papers began to appear. One of the earliest was the NORWICH POST in September 1701. The NORWICH GAZETTE (1706) The POSTMAN (1706) and the NORWICH MERCURY (1714) were soon

followed by the SUFFOLK MERCURY (1717) and the IPSWICH JOURNAL (1720). But they were not really local papers as we would understand them. There was hardly any local news. A man sat in an office waiting for the London papers to arrive on the stage coach, three times a week. Then, he set about choosing the most interesting items to publish in his 'local' paper. The DAILY COURANT, STANLEY'S NEWSLETTER, BOUCHER'S LETTER and others were raided for what might inform and entertain the reader.

Right from the word go, it had to be interesting or nobody would want to read it. That is why papers up to three hundred years old are still worth reading. Even some of the jokes haven't really changed that much through the years.

A gentleman, the other evening at a ball, being asked by a lady his opinion of her husband's picture set in a ring, observed he was no great judge of painting, but was happy to find her ladyship had a husband she could turn round her [little] finger.

IPSWICH JOURNAL January 25th 1777

A FISHY CYCLING STORY – *One of our cycling men did a bit of fishing in the river here the other day, and when he mounted his machine to return home, the handlebar was decorated with a handkerchief containing some remarkably fine eels. He didn't ride far before the tyre of his front wheel came off and when he got off his iron steed to investigate the amount of the damage, one of the largest eels glided out of the handkerchief and dropped onto the groove of the wheel, which it completely encircled, and stuck there . . . Our friend is a practical man and knows a good thing when he sees it. So, letting well alone, he stuck the tail of the eel in its mouth and rode home on his new tyre. The eel is not dead yet, and it is hoped with careful using, may last throughout the season.*
CROMER AND NORTH WALSHAM POST July 22nd 1899

Papers then, as now, could be brutal or heartwarming, sometimes even both.

On Monday, about sunrise, there happened the greatest overflowing of the sea, occasioned by a great spring tide. It made 17 breaches in the bank between Spalding and Wisbitch, and several hundreds of acres are overflowed. At Gedney, it has washed down the walls of several houses, especially that of Thomas Hay's the fisherman's and carried away all his household goods, he endeavouring to save none of them but his wife and a barrel of ale, to both of which he had been wedded about fifty years, he resolving to die with his cask. But the tide coming more stronger than he imagined, he maturely deliberated which of the two to let go of, in order to save himself; at last to his great grief he was forced to part with his beloved cask, and he and his wife were saved by a miracle.
IPSWICH GAZETTE February 28th 1736

CAVENDISH – *One day last week, a child about 12 months old, son of William Thompson, cabinet-maker, of this place, managed during the temporary absence of its mother, to fall head foremost into a pail of water. When found, the child's head was at the bottom of the pail and had probably been immersed several minutes, as, when extricated, breathing was quite suspended. Mr. Waring, surgeon, was, however, soon in attendance, and the proper remedies being used, animation was at length restored, but* *some time will probably elapse before the little sufferer quite recovers from the effects of the accident.*

WEST SUFFOLK AND NORTH ESSEX FREE PRESS
August 30th 1855

Though the language may seem a little old-fashioned, the reporting hasn't changed all that much. What you can read in this book are highlights from the papers of Suffolk and Norfolk as they brought the news to the people of East Anglia all those years ago.

Certain themes have proved popular with the reading public over the last three hundred years, and continue to do so. Whilst an editor cannot dictate what news falls on his desk, the kinds of tales that sold newspapers rapidly established themselves as favourites with the reading public.

Take, for example, love and marriage . . .

1

Love and marriage

Courting in the eighteenth and nineteenth centuries was a serious business, likely to lead to marriage, pregnancy or both, but not necessarily in that order.

A young physician who was in love with a fair patient but was unable from bashfulness to reveal his passion, wrote her a passionate declaration and left it on the table, where the servant, naturally enough, thought it was a prescription and took it to the Chemist's, who the next day sent it back to the poor doctor with apology that he was 'out of the ingredients necessary to make up what was wanted.'

FRAMLINGHAM WEEKLY NEWS
December 10th 1864

The WEST SUFFOLK AND NORTH ESSEX FREE PRESS for September 13th 1855 recounts a letter passing through Hereford Post Office

addressed *'For that girl, I don't no her name, they calls her "the galloper"*
and lives somewhere in Bowsy Lane, Hereford. Shure don't give this to any
girl but that girl.' The letter, we are told, reached its destination, as
the Hereford police were well acquainted with her nickname.

In Friday Street, Wapping, a poor woman was safely delivered of four
children, three boys and a girl on Sunday night last. What adds a little
to the singularity of this occurrence is they are all illegitimate and the
parish have compromised with the father for 20L on the presumption of
a single birth.

IPSWICH JOURNAL May 20th 1797

There were those who cut it exceedingly fine when they walked
up the aisle.

Last week a wedding was solemnized at a village near Stamford, which
was attended by some very singular circumstances – a young man having
paid his addresses to a female in the neighbourhood (for at least nine
months) it became requisite he should marry her. He accordingly sum-
moned his friends and relatives to be present at the consummation: this
being done, it was also necessary to send for another attendant, and he, no
less a person than the accoucheur.* Agreeable to the notice, friends, rela-
tives, and doctor attended. The lady being something easier, it was agreed
that they should proceed to church, which was only across the way, and
that the doctor should attend them, as it was not certain whose services
might be first wanted; but for decency, the doctor was stationed in the
porch of the church until the ceremony was over. One of the attendants,
brother to the bride, shewed, during the service, great anxiety, observing,
that if the parson was not quick, the child would be a bastard. The lady,
however, was not delivered of a fine girl until early the next morning.

BURY POST August 30th 1797

*Obstetrician

Even in 1736, the following letter from a barely literate servant to
her lover was seen as quaint, and an entertainment for the paper's
readers:

Lovin Der Charls,
This, with mi kind lov to yow,
is to tel yow, after al owr sport
and fun i am lik to pay fore; for
i am with Child, and where of
mi sister Nan knos it, and cals
me hore and bech, and is redy
to ter mi sol owt; and curs Jack
Penny kises her evry tim he
cums ashor, and the saci Dog
would hav lade with me to, but
i wold not let him, for i wil be
alwas honest to yow; therefor,
Der Charls, cum ashor, and let
us be mared to safe mi vartu;
and if you hav no munni, i wil
paun mi new stais, and sel mi
new smoks you gav me, and
that wil pay the parson, and
find us a diner and pray, Der

Lovin Chars, cum ashore; and, Der Charls, don't be frad for want of a
ring, for i have stol my sister Nans, and the nasty tod shal never hav it
no mor; for she tels about, that i am goin to have a basterd: and god bles
yowr lovin sol cum sune for i longs to be mared acordin to your promis,
and i will be your Der varius wife tel deth.

  Sarah Hartrop

Pray don't let your mesmat Jak se this, if yow do hel tel owr Nan, and shel
ter mi hart owt then, for she is a Devil at me now.

IPSWICH GAZETTE June 12th 1736

At least one local paper took a delight in embarrassing members of
its reading public by recounting tales of their misfortunes. Though
no name is mentioned, it could not have been very difficult for the
people of Wisbech to work out who was being ridiculed here:

WISBECH.   Cooling The Draper's Burning Love.

Our dapper young draper is not allowed to go to the house of his charmer, so he saw her home on Whit Monday evening, and arranged to see her at the back. He did so, and got on top the water butt, to have his good night kiss, when he, in the words of the poet, passionately recited :—

My darling ! I'm here according to time—
I wish I could get a bit higher ;
For to kiss you dear pet is always sublime :
And with love my heart is on fire.

Just at this moment the tub top gave way and in he went, up to his neck in water: this with a pummelling from his rival, will long make him remember Whitsuntide 1883.

HUNSTANTON TELEPHONE & WEST NORFOLK CHRONICLE May 18th 1883

In spite of all the problems, both sexes tried their hardest to find a mate. The IPSWICH AND COLCHESTER TIMES of April 8th 1859 referred to an act of 1770 which stated *'that women of whatever age, profession or degree, whether virgins, maids or widows that shall . . . impose upon, seduce and betray into matrimony any of his majesty's subjects by the scents, paints, cosmetic washes, artificial teeth, false hair . . . iron stays, high heeled shoes or bolstered hips shall incur the penalty of the law now in force against witchcraft and like misdemeanours and that the marriage, upon con-viction shall stand null and void.'* Oddly, the Witchcraft Act had been repealed in 1736.

And if a man needed a little encouragement, *'In Exeter there are no less than 27 widows who hold respectable inns or taverns'* (LYNN ADVERTISER April 25th 1843).

According to the LYNN ADVERTISER, in February 1843 just two valentines lay undelivered at Warrington, one addressed to *'The ugliest woman'* and another to *'The prettiest girl in Penbeth'.* The post-man did not want to be responsible for making the decision in either case.

> *On Valentine's Day, the Twopenny post had such an extraordinary influx of letters and valentines from the lads and lasses, that the postmen, although assisted by a number of supernumeraries, could not get through their deliveries in regular time. At the receiving house, in New Street, Covent Garden, near 1,000 valentines were put into the box.*
>
> IPSWICH JOURNAL February 18th 1804

According to the SUFFOLK AND ESSEX FREE PRESS in 1866, over three thousand letters passed through Sudbury Post Office on the morning of Valentine's Day that year. This and other such tradi-tions were established early.

> *A person contrived to forestall and monopolise the whole of the mistletoe in Covent Garden market last week, by which it is supposed he cleared of 400L, having sold it three times higher than the usual price, the girls insisting on it at any rate, that they might enjoy a free trade in kissing.*
>
> BURY & NORWICH POST December 31st 1800

Then, when the right match had been agreed, it was off to church.

> *On Tuesday last was married Mr. Philip Dikes of Pettistree to Miss Gross, of Rendlesham, an agreeable young lady with a genteel fortune.*
>
> IPSWICH JOURNAL October 9th 1784

The union between the young Earl of Oxford and the beautiful Miss Scott is fixed for the first week in February. This young lady, who is one of 19 children, of a respectable Hampshire clergyman, was fortunate enough to make this conquest at a ball, last Summer, in Southampton.

IPSWICH JOURNAL January 25th 1794

On Monday last was married at Hickling in Norfolk, Simon Greenacre of that parish aged 74, and Hannah Corbet of the same parish, his fifth wife, aged 61. That he might not be encumbered with the demands of her for her former husband's creditors, he took her, quite naked, at one of the principal crossways of the parish, after which they went to church, where the ceremony was performed. The road leading from his house to the church, which is upwards of half a mile, was strewn with flowers.

IPSWICH JOURNAL May 1764

NEWCASTLE – *In Christmas holidays was married at Allendale town, Thomas Thirtlewell, aged 82, to Hannah Graham, aged 40, being his third wife. After the ceremony . . . the bridegroom got so fuddled that he was obliged to be supported by two men to his house . . . next morning, he asked his bride if they were married . . . and could hardly be convinced till she shewed him his hat with the ribbon in it.*

NORWICH MERCURY January 29th 1773

But the ceremony did not always go to plan.

BUNGAY – A SCENE IN CHURCH – *On Sunday morning last, the congregation of a small parish church not very far from this town were much startled on hearing from the further end of the building, the words 'I forbid!' after the banns of marriage for the second time had been announced in the usual way by the rector, and their surprise was increased when they found that it was the voice of the young intended bridegroom. Of course, the cause for this change of mind became the subject of village gossip and enquiry, and we are informed that it arose from some difference of opinion as to the value of sundry articles of furniture which he had purchased.*

SUFFOLK CHRONICLE January 2nd 1864

On Sunday morning, a young couple attended at St. Nicholas Church, Yarmouth, to be married, accompanied by the parents of the bride, all of them being in a respectable sphere of life. Before the ceremony commenced, the young lady burst into a loud titter, and notwithstanding the reproof of the Rev. E. Pellew, who officiated, she made no endeavours to restrain her laughter. The Minister, justly displeased with her levity, broke off in the midst of the service and dismissed the happy couple, half married, at the same time informing the lady that if she presented herself at the altar on Monday in a more serious and becoming frame of mind, he would not object to finish the ceremony.

St Nicholas' church, Great Yarmouth

SUFFOLK CHRONICLE August 23rd 1834

Of course, the wedding was only half of the process, as this sad story indicates:

We have advice from Aston upon Trent in Derbyshire that one John Bodger of that town being told by some of his neighbours of his intended marriage with one Dorothy King, an alehouse keeper's daughter of the same place, he in a seeming derision of her mean parentage, made this rash wish that if ever he took her to be his wife he wished the same day he was married to her, he might either brake his neck or be drowned. Not withstanding this and many other sad expressions to the same purpose, he was married to the said young woman soon after. But on the wedding day, at night staying at Shardley, a town about a mile distant from his house, drinking and making merry very late, and it being a very dark night, the bridegroom, then much disordered with liquor, and riding homeward with his company, was separated from them, was lost and could not be heard of till the next morning, when his horse coming home with his bridle and saddle, it gave suspicion that he was drowned; so that searching the River Trent about Willen Ferry, they found him drowned according to his rash wish, his body lying among the flags and rushes. His bride hearing of this sad disaster remains in great sorrow and affliction; but tho' lawfully married to him, 'tis thought she will hardly recover any part of his estate by reason she was deprived of the usual happiness of being bedded as well as wedded.

IPSWICH JOURNAL August 12th 1721

On Friday last, the complaint of Mrs. S. was opened against her husband in a great ecclesiastical court. The principal charge brought against him was that he was incapable of performing matrimonial rites according to the law of nature . . . Mr. S. denies her charge and will submit to a scrutiny of the faculty.

NORWICH MERCURY February 16th 1721

After marriage, a woman's rights were much restricted and the husband was expected to be the boss. A woman was, after all, supposed to know her place. The word 'sexist' hadn't even been invented but plenty soon learnt that marriage was far from the ideal they had expected.

THE BEST SEWING MACHINE — *The very best sewing machine a man can have is a wife. It is one that requires but a kind word to set it in motion, rarely gets out of repair, makes but little noise, is seldom the cause of dust, and, once in motion, will go on uninterruptedly for hours, without the slightest trimming or the smallest personal supervision being necessary. It will make shirts, darn stockings, sew on buttons, mark pocket handkerchiefs, cut out pinafores, and manufacture children's frocks out of*

any old thing you can give it; and this it will do behind your back just as well as before your face. In short, no gentleman's establishment is complete without one of these sewing machines in the house.

IPSWICH AND COLCHESTER TIMES March 25th 1859

Under the headline MATRIMONIAL COERCION, the SUFFOLK CHRONICLE for March 1817 described how, at Lincoln Assizes, William Nubert and his wife Ann were tried for burglary. Though William tried his hardest to convince the court that his wife had persuaded him to do it, it was presumed in law that the husband must be master of his own home and therefore the Jury acquitted the wife and found William Nubert guilty.

Unhappy marriages could result in any number of different outcomes.

A few days ago, a sailor, who had been abroad about three years, coming on shore, went to his house, where he had left a young wife. When

Ships in dock at Yarmouth

he came in, he found her sitting by the fire with a child in her lap, and a man sitting on a chair by her, who said to the woman, 'shew the gentleman into a room' (it being a public house). Jack asked her if she did not know him; and where she had got that child. She replied, 'why, dear Jack, I thought you were dead, and I am married again.' 'Married!' 'Aye,' says the second husband.

'Very well,' says Jack, 'but I married her first and by G—d I'll have her whilst I am on shore, and you may be her husband whilst I am at sea, and I'll pay half to maintain the children.'

They came soon to an amicable understanding, and the second husband is now drawer to his wife, hoping Jack will soon sail, that he might be landlord again.

IPSWICH JOURNAL March 8th 1777

A man named Kelly was charged with having hurled at the head of his wife an iron trivet. His defence was that it did not hit her, the door having happily interposed between it and the object of his violence. Though he claimed her aggravating tongue was impossible to bear, he was bound over to keep the peace.

SUFFOLK CHRONICLE January 21st 1837

A person in this town having long suspected the fidelity of his wife fell upon the following scheme to get at the fact. Yesterday se'nnight he pretended that business called him into the country, and that he should not return till the next day; at the same time took care that the man should be informed of it like wise. About midnight he returned. In going upstairs the back way, he heard a whispering in the chamber, upon which he immediately rushed in with a brace of pistols in his hand, and desired his wife to strike a light, for that something had happened that occasioned his return sooner than he expected. The wife let fall the matches, and requested her husband to go down for some, as she could not find them, or to let her go; but the husband would do neither; and mentioning the word 'pistols' if she stirred, threw the man in the bed into such a panic, that he got out and jumped from the chamber window (which is about 16 ft from the ground) with only his shirt on, leaving his breeches (in which were 16 guineas, and papers of consequence in his pocket book) behind him, which he has never yet since been to claim.

The husband being thus deprived of his revenge upon the man, his wife felt the more of it, perhaps, than he otherwise would have done, for after having flogged her, he turned her quite naked into the street. However, the husband appears satisfied with the transaction, thinking himself, probably, very well satisfied for the dishonour done to his bed. The man received much hurt in jumping out of the window; he was confined to his bed several days, and now is very lame.

IPSWICH JOURNAL August 22nd 1778

Richard King of Harwich gave notice in the IPSWICH JOURNAL of September 24th 1763 that he and Elizabeth his wife 'are lately parted by mutual agreement and have agreed to live separate from each other'. However, he warned all persons not to trust his wife on his account.

For the poor, an unhappy marriage was something they were probably stuck with, but the wealthy manged their marital affairs like their estates and their businesses. Failure could result in litigation. When Lord Paget conducted what was to become a very public extra-marital affair with Lady Caroline Wellesley in 1809, it led to a duel with her brother and a settlement of £20,000 to her husband, the brother of the Duke of Wellington. The case was pursued with much the same vigour as the tabloid press might use today. But then, if a husband tired of his wife, he could always sell her.

Thursday, a butcher at Halstead sold his wife to a wealthy farmer in that neighbourhood for three guineas and a good supper; the woman acceding to the bargain, the farmer immediately took her home and seemed very well pleased with his purchase.

IPSWICH JOURNAL February 8th 1777

A farmer of the parish of Stowupland sold his wife to a neighbour for five guineas, and being happy to think he had made a good bargain, presented her with a guinea to buy her a new gown; he then went to Stowmarket, and gave orders for the bells to be rung upon the occasion.

IPSWICH JOURNAL January 28th 1787
(This date was given by John Glyde
in his book 'A New Suffolk Garland'
but appears to be incorrect.)

ABUSE OF MARRIAGE — *On Friday a coal-porter exhibited his wife in Smithfield with a halter round her neck for sale; he demanded a guinea for her, but hung on hand for some time, until a man of good appearance made the purchase, and packing her, halter and all, into a Hackney-coach, drove for Blackfriars Bridge, amidst the huzzas of the mob.*

SUFFOLK CHRONICLE November 28th 1801

A man living at Alfreton has been showing signs of jealousy at his wife's apparently too friendly disposition towards the son of the person in whose house they lodged. While the parties were drinking together on Saturday, however, the husband seems to have looked at the matter in another light and offered to sell his wife to the young man for a glass of ale.

The offer was accepted, the glass of ale was provided and the lady, readily falling in with the arrangement, took off her wedding ring and from that time considered herself the property of the purchaser.

THETFORD & WATTON TIMES & PEOPLE'S JOURNAL May 6th 1882

A butcher being in company at Newmarket with a tanner who always bought his skins, agreed to sell his wife to him at 5½d a lb, the money to be paid the following Tuesday on her delivery. The agreement was drawn up by an eminent attorney and the tanner deposited one guinea in part payment.

NORFOLK CHRONICLE 1770

In a court case of 1752, it was left to the court to decide just who was the guilty party in a severe case of domestic violence. Thomas Halwyn had charged Catherine, his wife, and her two sons by a previous marriage, with beating him. They were brought from the cells to answer the charges. Halwyn swore to the court:

May it please your worship, this woman my wife is a very sober discreet woman . . . when she does not take a cup or so, for indeed when she does, she is the veriest balragger on the face of the earth . . . oftener than it should be, she flies upon me like any dragoness . . . and then her two sons take her part and yesterday they all fell upon me and beat my poor head into a mummy, or a jelly as a man may say.

NORWICH MERCURY February 1st 1752

Unfortunately for him, his neighbours saw it very differently, testifying how badly Thomas Halwyn had treated his wife. As a result, the three accused were released, and he was sent to gaol in their place.

A QUARRELSOME OLD COUPLE – *Mary Harvey, an old lady of perhaps 60 summers was charged by her aged spouse* [at Halesworth Petty Sessions] *Isaac Harvey of Wissett, who appeared before the bench supported by crutches and whose appearance suggested anything but a strong constitution, with having . . . assaulted him by pulling him violently to the ground – treatment not becoming her years nor her station as the wife of an aged and feeble old man. From the evidence, it appeared very evident that – to use an old phrase – 'the grey mare was the better horse.' . . . The Chairman recommended them to go home and live together on more amicable terms.*

HALESWORTH TIMES May 19th 1857

Great Ashfield church

Some people seem to have liked marriage so much, they did it more than once, even when they shouldn't.

BIGAMY — *T. Crane was indicted for having feloniously intermarried at Bury St. Edmunds with Ann Copsey, his wife Elizabeth, to whom he was married at Ashfield in Suffolk, being still alive. The case was clearly proved by the testimony of the second wife and the persons who were present at the first marriage. It was also proved that the first wife was now alive.*

The prisoner stated in his defence that he had received a letter from his first wife stating that she was dead, and believing her to speak the truth he had taken unto him a second wife.

The Jury, however, under the learned Judge's directions, found the prisoner guilty. He was fined one shilling and discharged.

SUFFOLK CHRONICLE March 22nd 1817

A man in North Carolina, at different times, married 13 wives and a reward was offered for his apprehension. A person anxious to bring this monster to justice enticed him into his house and persuaded his wife to chat with him until he could procure a constable. When he returned, he

found the culprit had eloped with the lady.
LYNN ADVERTISER September 13th 1842

Judges had widely differing views as to the criminality of bigamy: the sentencing could vary from a low fine to transportation. But marriage was still regarded as an essential part of life for many.

Last Sunday night, an eminent broker not far from Moorfields buried his wife and on Tuesday was married to her aunt. It is generally said he changed his condition so suddenly because he could not lye without a bedfellow.
NORWICH MERCURY March 30th 1745

Last week, a most extraordinary circumstance took place at Surfleet. A woman of that town named Pinder was actually married to a man named Newman before the body of her former husband was laid in the grave.
SUFFOLK CHRONICLE May 13th 1815

For the most part, the reporters and editors of our local papers were men, and they shared many a good tale with their male readers at the expense of women, and wives in particular.

A gentleman had a horse that started and broke his wife's neck: a neighbouring squire told him he wished to purchase it for his wife to ride upon. 'No,' says the other — 'I will not sell that little fellow, because I intend to marry again myself.'
WEST SUFFOLK AND NORTH ESSEX FREE PRESS June 12th 1856

SEEING A MAN HOME – *I picked Simmons up pretty near dead drunk and took him home. When I got to his house, as I thought, I shook him a bit and said, 'Here you are.' 'Right,' said he and gave a big bang at the knocker. Up went a window. 'Who's there?' screamed a woman. 'I have brought the old man home,' said I. 'All right,' she cried and came to the door. She immediately seized hold of old Simmons and gave him such a shaking that his teeth seemed to rattle in his head. 'Who are you shaking of?' said he. 'Goodness gracious,' cried the woman. 'That is not my husband's voice.'*

I struck a match . . . 'There,' said the woman, 'I've been sitting up here expecting my husband home drunk, and now I've wasted my strength on a stranger.'

'Don't he live here?' said I.

'No' said the woman, 'he don't.'

'What made you knock?' said I to Simmons.

'Knock,' said he. 'You told me to.'

'I thought you lived here.'

'Glad I don't,' said he.

At last I found where he did live and got him home. Mrs Simmons was waiting up for him. 'Oh,' says she – 'You're the wretch as makes my poor husband drunk are you?' And she caught me a slap across the face. I have never seen a drunken man home since.

DOWNHAM MARKET GAZETTE January 3rd 1880

By a series of interesting experiments lately made in Philadelphia, a woman's tongue has been capable of moving 1,920 times in a minute. Think of that and weep.

DISS EXPRESS April 6th 1866

Not long ago, a premium was offered by an Agricultural Society for the best mode of irrigation, and the latter word by mistake of the printer, having been changed to 'irritation', a farmer sent his wife to gain the prize.

STOWMARKET COURIER September 23rd 1869

Woman: Did you know you talk in your sleep?

Husband: It's the only chance I get.

THETFORD WEEKLY POST April 12th 1906

But this next story has everything. It is the stuff of old folk-songs and bar-room ballads. And it entertained our fore-fathers two hundred and fifty years ago. The IPSWICH JOURNAL for March 22nd 1760 published the beginning of what was to become an amazing story:

Sometime in October last was married Samuel Bundy (aged about 20 years, apprentice to Mr. Angel, near the Almshouses Christchurch Surrey) to Mary Parlour of the said parish: upon Bundy's telling his bride he had lately contracted a bad distemper, she waited with patience till about the middle of last week when some of the neighbours thought proper to make a strict search upon which they found the bridegroom to be a perfect female . . . she acknowledges she has acted the bully at bad houses, her behaviour was singular in playing with and kissing the girls and was high in the esteem of many.

The following week, this more complete account appeared:

Yesterday a young woman in man's apparel was committed to Southwark Bridwell by Justice Clark for farther examination, by the name of Samuel Bundy, for defrauding a young woman of money and apparel by marrying of her. The following account the prisoner gives of herself: she says she is twenty years of age, that seven years since she was seduced from her mother (who then and now, lives near Smithfield) by a limner who debauched her; that the day after, to avoid the pursuit of her mother, or any discovery of her should any advertisement appear, he dressed her in boy's apparel and adopted her for his son, by the above name; with him she was a year; at length they separated and she took one voyage to sea which kept her employed more than twelve months, in which voyage she performed the several duties of a sailor; that some time after she came from sea, she bound herself to Mr. Angel, a painter in the parish of Christchurch, Surrey. With him she continued a year, lying with her master when they were in the country at work, and that without the least discovery whatsoever. Whilst with Mr. Angel she was taken notice of by a young woman, who lived at the King's head in Gravel Lane, Southwark, to whom she was duly married at a neighbouring church near six months since. Quitting her master upon some dispute between them, she was obliged to depend upon her wife for support, who expended her money and pawned her clothes for her mate's maintenance, which is the fraud she is charged with. The adopted husband says the wife soon discovered the mistake she had made, but was determined for some time not to expose the matter. Since marriage, she entered on board the Prince Frederick man-of-war at Chatham, but ran away from it for fear the great number of hands of board should discover her sex.

She afterwards entered on board a merchant ship with about twenty hands which (she says) she approved of much, but ran away from that to return to the wife, whom (she says) she dearly loves; and there seems a strong love or friendship on the other side as she keeps the prisoner company in her confinement. The prisoner makes a very good figure as a man, and in her proper dress cannot fail of being a very agreeable woman.

IPSWICH JOURNAL March 29th 1760

Saucy stories were one thing, but I must admit this rhyme in a NORFOLK CHRONICLE of 1777 came as a bit of a surprise.

The night he was wedded, quoth Inigo Jones,
Thou flesh of my flesh and thou bone of my bones,
There's a joke in the name of thy husband, sweet Nancy,
A rare one, so rare that it tickles my fancy:
Lie still, my dear love, and my good thing shall out –
Oh Lord, Mr. Jones, what are you about?
Hush, hush, pretty creature, your squeaking and moans,
'Tis the joke that I told you of, In I Go Jones.

The NORFOLK CHRONICLE in 1780 reported the story of a local dignitary who was so keen to put a stop to marriages where the bride was already 'big with child' that he offered to present a silver breastplate, valued 10s to any bride under 25 whose first child was not born until 9 months after the wedding. She was to wear it each time she came to church. It would be inscribed with the words 'The Reward of Chastity'. We were led to believe there was not exactly a rush of takers.

2

Entertainment

For many, life was quite monotonous, so anything out of the ordinary was worth writing and reading about. The Ipswich Journal of May 1st 1824 carried a long advertisement announcing the visit of Wombwell's Menagerie during St. George's Fair in Ipswich. This travelling zoo was described as having *'the largest number of animals collected together since the days of Noah'*, and included *'the pelican of the wilderness'.*

Wombwell is a name that would appear for well over a hundred years in articles and adverts, as readers of my other books of newspaper stories will recognise. George Wombwell gained a reputation as a breeder of exotic animals. Local papers in June 1841 reported the birth of five lion-cubs at his menagerie while it was in the area, adding that he had bred over 120 lions in captivity by that time.

There could, of course, be a darker side to such exhibitions as he might arrange:

A fight between a bull and one of Mr. Wombwell's Lions, lately exhibited at Ipswich, is expected to take place in the course of the Easter week at Newmarket.

SUFFOLK CHRONICLE June 30th 1819

On Wednesday, Wombwell's menagerie left Yarmouth, and in proceeding over Rollesby Bridge, the large caravan containing the elephants partially broke down, plunging the colossal animals in a cold bath. With the assistance of a number of men and 28 horses, they were, after considerable delay, again placed safely on terra firma.

LYNN ADVERTISER February 15th 1842

We find adverts for Madame Tussaud's touring East Anglia a number of times, plus the predictable run of freak shows and child prodigies.

Last week, one David Fearn came to this town and has taken up residence in Kennedy's Close. He was born in the Shire of Ross, aged 26, is about

THIS is to give Notice to all Gentlemen, Ladies, and Others, That there is brought to this Place, and is to be shown at the Lower Half-Moon in the Market-place in Norwich, by the Woman that bore them, (as is attested by Dr. Stud of Saxmundham in Suffolk, who deliver'd her the 25th of June last) one of the greatest Curiosities in Nature, being a Double Foetus of a BOY and GIRL, join'd together in the following Manner: The Bodies grow together, so as to seem but one; from which proceeds two Heads and Necks, in full Proportion; between which arises one Arm, without Hand or Finger, and another on each Side in their proper Places; also two Legs and Feet, with Toes compleat, in their proper Situation; and from the hinder Part of the Body, proceeds a Leg and Foot, with six Toes: There is Distinctions of each Sex very plain, and but one Anus and Navel common to both. To be seen at any Time, from Eight in the Morning till Ten in the Evening, without Loss of Time. N. B. Gentlemen and Ladies that are curious, may have it carry'd to their own Houses in any Part of the City. giving an Hour's Notice; it will likewise be carry'd to any Club of Gentlemen in an Evening. giving the same Notice as above. It is in as full Proportion, as a Child half a Year old.

This advert from the NORWICH MERCURY (September 1736) has to be one of the most tasteless ones we have encountered.

30 inches high, yet 35 inches round, has all the human members, only his hands resemble the feet of a seal, and his feet those of a bear, and can dance a hornpipe to admiration.

SUFFOLK GAZETTE January 10th 1736

We hear that the tall woman, Christian Godwin, from Essex, who has had the honour of being seen by most of the nobility and gentry at Charing Cross for some time, designs very speedily to make a tour round England. She is seven foot high, and proportional to her height, tho' but eighteen years of age. She has had the pleasure of giving satisfaction to everybody whose curiosity have led 'em to see her.

SUFFOLK GAZETTE June 5th 1736

Freak show stars were often the celebrities of their day. When Daniel Lambert died at the age of 39, weighing over 52 stone, the IPSWICH JOURNAL used the following words in tribute:

Mr. BLAKER,
The Modern Living COLOSSUS
Or Wonderful
GIANT,
Is to be seen at the BEAR in the Market-Place, NORWICH.

THIS Phœnomenon in Nature hath already had the Honour of being inspected by great Numbers of the Nobility and Gentry, by many of the Royal Society, and by several Gentlemen and Ladies who are Lovers of natural Curiosities; who allow him to be of a stupendous Height, and esteem him the best proportion'd of his Size they ever saw.

Nature had endured all the trespass she could admit: the poor man's corpulency had constantly increased until the clogged machinery of life stood still and this prodigy of mammon was numbered with the dead.

IPSWICH JOURNAL
July 1st 1809

His death caused a huge problem for the hotel where he died. A wall had to be taken down to remove the corpse and it took 20 men to lower him into his grave. Only a few days earlier, he had been weighed using the *'world famous Caledonian balance owned by Mr. King of Ipswich'* and was found to weigh nearly 53 stone.

At the other end of the scale, the YARMOUTH INDEPENDENT reported the wedding of 'Tom Thumb (real name: Charles. S. Stratton) to a *'miniature lady',* Lavinia Warren, in February 1863. She stood just 32 inches high, an inch shorter than her husband. Seats at the church were sold for 75 dollars for four. General Tom Thumb toured East Anglia, as newspaper adverts show.

> *A blind child, only three years old, son of Mr. Laud* at Orford in Suffolk, plays upon the spinnet, harpsichord and organ, several tunes, and in regular chords, to the astonishment even of musical performers. The babe will perform in Bungay and Beccles in midsummer week and upon the Tower church organ at Ipswich on the three race days in the following week between the hours of eleven and one. He will afterwards be at Hadleigh, Stowmarket, Bury, Sudbury and Eye. It is humbly hoped he will obtain the attention, approbation and encouragement of ladies, gentlemen and others.*
>
> IPSWICH JOURNAL 1782

*Mr Laud was organist at Orford Church.

> *A child, 6 years of age, being introduced into company for his extraordinary abilities, was asked by an eminent dignified clergyman where God was, with the proffered reward of an orange. 'Tell me,' replied the boy, 'where He is not and I will give you two.'*
>
> NORFOLK CHRONICLE February 4th 1792

However, star quality could always be recognised.

> *It is reported that when the Countess of Coventry was at Worcester, such was the adoration of the low people towards that amazing beauty, that upon their hearing a shoemaker in town had been honoured with taking her measure for a pair of shoes, they flocked to his house and paid a penny each to see her shoe, and before the shoes were finished the fellow had got upwards of 2 guineas in pence.*
>
> IPSWICH JOURNAL August 1st 1752

POSITIVELY THE LAST DAY.

UNDER THE PATRONAGE OF HER MAJESTY,
THE ROYAL FAMILY, and the
PRINCIPAL CROWNED HEADS OF EUROPE

RARE COMBINATION OF NOVELTIES.

GENERAL TOM THUMB!
PICCO!!

SENOR OLIVEIRA, First Violinist to the Queen
of Spain;
MR. WILLIAM TOMLIN,
The Celebrated Baritone, from the nobility's concerts,
London; together with

OTHER RARE MUSICAL NOVELTIES!
Forming a combination of elevated and delightful attractions seldom witnessed.

LECTURE HALL, IPSWICH,

SATURDAY, APRIL 23, and positively no longer.

THREE ENTERTAINMENTS from Twelve to
Half-past One, Three to Half-past Four, and Eight to
Half-past Nine o'clock. Doors open half an hour
previous.

DAY ENTERTAINMENT——Admission: Reserved
Seats, 2s.; Unreserved Seats, 1s.; Children under Ten
years of age half-price. Schools liberally received.

EVENING ENTERTAINMENT—Admission: Reserved Seats, 2s.; Unreserved, 1s,; Back Seats, 6d. Children half-price to Reserved and Unreserved Seats only.

G. A. WELLS, MANAGER.
T. H. JOHN, AGENT.

ANNUAL BURY GALA!
MONDAY, JULY 22ND, 1889.

BOTANIC GARDENS, BURY ST. EDMUND'S.

BURY FREE PRESS July 1889

Performers could be found, most days, in the streets of our towns, though they were not always appreciated. John Batto, an itinerant professor of inspiring music applied to the magistrates for their permission to *'go about the good town of Ipswich delighting the inhabitants with the melody of sweet sounds'.* Batto was known to travel about the kingdom with drum, tambourine, fiddle and sundry other well known musical instruments. Though he argued his case strongly, the magistrates feared that the *'sweet power of his music might accomplish the undesirable feat of frightening the horses into a pace somewhat more rapid than might be consistent with the safety of passengers.'* The application was refused and the disconsolate musician *'retired surprised and indignant at the lack of musical taste evinced by the Ipswich authorities'* (SUFFOLK CHRONICLE January 21st 1837).

What was classed by some as entertainment was far from acceptable to others even 250 years ago:

The Custom of throwing at cocks so much practised at Shrovetide and which is so opposite to every divine and human law, will, we hear, by the united endeavours of the magistrates to be totally extirpated . . . it is hoped that all parents and masters will prevent their children, servants and apprentices from indulging themselves in this barbarous diversion . . . which tends to instill the disposition of savages into the breasts of Christians.

NORWICH MERCURY February 28th 1756

THIS is to give Notice, That there will be a Match of Cock fought at the new erected Pitt at the White-Elm in Cobdock near Ipfwich, on Tuef-day and Wednefday the 17th and 18th of this Inftant, between Suffolk and Effex, for two Guineas a Battle, and eight Guineas the odd Battle. Where all Lovers of that Diverfion will meet with good Accommodation and an hearty Welcome.
JAMES HOWES.

IPSWICH GAZETTE *April 14th 1733*

Far better some good clean fun:

THE GREASY POLE AT HUNSTANTON REGATTA.

The greatest fun of the day was trying to walk the Greasy Pole put up about 200 yards from the shore. A young lady (a pupil of Tennyson's) sends us a short poem on the subject.

Slippery sloppery slip, then dip;
Uppery again to the top;
Againery thenery they'd try to walk,
But down into the sea they'd pop.

Slippery sloppery slide they tried
Againery to cross the pole;
But Wiggleum waggleum down they came,
And repeatedly made a big hole.

HUNSTANTON TELEPHONE September 15th 1882

3
Rich and poor

Those reading the papers were, by and large, well off. However, they seem to have taken a delight in reading about those at the foot of the social scale. The Ipswich Journal for June 16th 1804 estimated that in London there were 15,000 beggars. But they could be found nearer home than that.

A beggar man, apparently very old and in great distress, with a child in his arms came into a Public House on Friday evening and begged alms with great earnestness. A young man in the house at the time, suspecting that he was an imposter, took hold of the child, when immediately, the head came off and discovered it to be made of plaster of Paris. After shaking the old man a little, an old red wig fell off and discovered him to be a young man, about thirty. He begged very hard to get off, without asking damages for the loss of his child, and was turned out of the house.

Ipswich Journal August 4th 1827

Peter O'Brien was convicted as a rogue and vagabond for begging in the parish of Ramsholt, and pretending to have been struck by lightning. He was given three months hard labour.

Bury Gazette July 28th 1824

Wednesday last, Thomas Ward Holl was committed to Wymondham Bridewell, as a rogue and vagabond – he was apprehended near Filby

in this county in the character of a wounded mariner having lost his left arm, which, on examination, was found perfect. He was formerly an occupant of Dereham and has by his abandoned life spent a considerable sum of money.

NORFOLK CHRONICLE May 10th 1788

On Tuesday, one Peter James, a poor man aged 87 years, one of the city's scavengers, was run over by a dung-cart near St. Benedict's Gates, which crushed out one of his eyes. Otherwise, he was terribly bruised, of which he languished and then expired.

NORWICH MERCURY January 4th 1772

The plight of the poor in the two centuries before 1900 was particularly hard on children. They worked long hours from an early age and could encounter the very worst of experiences.

Early yesterday morning as a chimney sweeper was sweeping a chimney at Mr. Boyd's the Woolpack at Paddington, about halfway the chimney the boy met with an obstruction and putting his hand up to feel what stopt him took hold of the leg of a man which frighten'd him so much he came down immediately and could scarce be kept from going into fits: immediately after, the body of a man, quite smoked dry, tumbled down. By the appearance it made, it must have been there several months and is thought to have been some thief that endeavoured to come down the chimney to rob the house.

NORWICH MERCURY June 26th 1732

Throughout the 18th century, boys were sent up the chimneys to clean them, and on occasions, to put out fires. The IPSWICH JOURNAL of October 1st 1783 described a case in Broad Street London where *'a poor little fellow was so miserably burnt that he died the same night'.* As we know, great efforts were made by reformers to improve the lives of these children, but it was a long hard struggle.

CLIMBING BOYS — *The bill before the House of Commons for 'the better regulation of chimney sweepers and their apprentices, and for preventing the employment of boys in climbing chimneys' states 'that*

the necessity of employing such apprentices to cleanse chimneys by climbing them no longer exists in consequence of the invention of various machines for the purpose.'

SUFFOLK CHRONICLE
February 21st 1818

Whilst this law sought to protect children from the abuses of the past, it recognised that a proportion of flues could only be reached by sending boys up chimneys. This was still to be allowed, we were told, but only under strict regulation. Reformist papers like the SUFFOLK CHRONICLE and the NORWICH MERCURY gave this their strong support, as did the more influential local people such as the Gurneys, a Norwich Quaker banking family, and the Alexanders, their Suffolk equivalent.

However, the SUFFOLK CHRONICLE for May 3rd 1864 (Sup.) brought the public's attention to the fact that boys and girls were still being used to climb and clean chimneys in spite of legislation having been passed against it. The YARMOUTH GAZETTE in March 1875 reported the case of William Wyer, a master chimney-sweep who was sentenced to six months' hard labour at Cambridge Assizes for causing the death of a boy whom he had sent into a chimney flue, where he suffocated. Appalling cases of abuse and neglect of children were regularly reported throughout this time.

INQUISITION — *An inquest was held at Woodbridge on the body of M. K. Grayson aged five weeks. It appeared in evidence that the child's* *mother Mrs. Grayson had been in the habit of giving her children Laudanum to quiet them when cross and restless. On Monday evening last, she went to Chapel, having cautioned her servant girl not to give the baby Laudanum on any account; the infant, however, becoming cross, the girl to quiet her gave her a few drops mixed with sugar and water, when it was immediately taken ill and died about eight o'clock on the following morning. At the parents' request, the body was opened by a medical man who proved the quantity of Laudanum given to have caused its death. Great blame being attached to the mother, the Jury returned a verdict that the infant died from the effects of the drug administered through ignorance.*

SUFFOLK CHRONICLE August 24th 1833

MATCHES

In a similarly tragic case a child named John Able died at Heigham in Norfolk in 1846.

The child's mother on the previous Saturday perceived that it was taken with a violent purg-ing and sickness which induced her to apply to a neighbour, Mrs. Armes of the Cow & Hare Public House, who gave her a mixture containing a portion of Laudanum as a remedy. A few days afterwards, the child was taken ill and died.

NORFOLK NEWS
August 15th 1846

Abuse of such substances was not restricted to children, nor simply to the poor. On July 7th 1894, the EASTERN

DAILY PRESS recorded the death of Edward Allen, the proprietor of the White Lion Hotel at Eye, whilst on holiday at Great Yarmouth. He had overdosed on laudanum. The THETFORD & WATTON TIMES on January 14th 1882 spoke of the death of Emma Murrell of Norwich, who had died, aged 78, *'from excessive opium eating'*. It was said *'she had been in the habit all her life'*. The STOWMARKET COURIER, as late as September 1869, was reporting on child deaths from the phosphorous used in the manufacture of Lucifer matches. Poverty and ignorance was responsible for a good deal of suffering.

> **OVERCROWDING AT A HOUSE AT COMBS** — *At Stowmarket petty sessions, William Eastwick was charged by the sanitary Inspector with an offence under the Nuisance Act. With his wife and four children he lived in a room 11 feet by 11 and in a very filthy state. All looked sickly and unhealthy.*
>
> NORTH NORFOLK & YARMOUTH CONSTITUTIONALIST
> August 31st 1872

> **CORONER'S COURT — NORWICH** — *A woman named Matilda Henry died from lockjaw as a result of treading on a nail, which penetrated her foot. She handed the nail to her daughter remarking, 'If you grease the nail, the wound will heal.' Nothing was done for the injury and the woman died. The Coroner said he was surprised that such superstition should be believed.*
>
> Published in local papers and the DAILY MAIL July 15th 1902

Many families throughout the eighteenth and nineteenth centuries were dependent on charity and handouts. A measure of philanthropy was more or less expected of the better off.

> *On Christmas Eve was distributed to the poor of Holkham by order of Thomas William Coke Esq., ninety stone of beef and six combs of wheat: a great relief in this severe season.*
>
> NORFOLK CHRONICLE January 1777

The same newspaper that winter reported countless gifts including coals, red herrings, loaves, broth and even a forty-stone bullock. The

Duke of Grafton had given money to the poor of Thetford and Mrs Fakenham, on retiring as prison governess at Norwich, had given 22 prisoners a shilling and a quart of beer each.

Infant mortality was very high throughout the time covered by this book. By way of example, the IPSWICH JOURNAL regularly listed the burial statistics for East Anglian towns. In the last week in June 1755, the total burials in Norwich amounted to 39, of whom 22 were below ten years of age. This was typical.

As regards cruel treatment of children, not only the poor suffered. It was reported in the NORFOLK CHRONICLE for December 1858 that complaints had been made regarding the form of punishment used

at a Norwich School. This was known as *'shelving'* and the paper described how *'boys guilty of minor offences are placed for hours between shelves so they cannot stand upright, but are obliged to stoop until the head is brought nearly level with the knees'.* Dr Vincent, the headmaster, claimed this was a normal and valid form of punishment.

According to the SUFFOLK CHRONICLE of May 10th 1839, severe treatment was being imposed for trivial offences at Yarmouth Charity School. In this article, a young girl, for removing her cap whilst attending church for the third time that day, was beaten and sent through the streets chained to a log.

Mind you, the education on offer at some schools was of very doubtful quality. The SEARCHER OR NORFOLK AND SUFFOLK HUMOURIST, which described itself as a fashionable gazette of high and low life, included the following item in its first edition in 1839:

> *At a village school in Suffolk is the following inscription – 'Children tote to rede and plain work at 2 pens a week. For them as larns manners, 2 pens a week moor.'*

As the nineteenth century progressed, improving literacy amongst the masses became more of an issue, though it was not always well received.

John Pickrell was charged with neglecting to send his 12 year-old daughter, Mary Adderson, to school at Brancaster. His wife stated they had adopted the child who was an orphan, but they also had to support her husband's father aged 90, so the child sometimes had to remain at home to look after him as they lived in an isolated position and she had to go in search of livelihood. The case was dismissed, the parents promising to send her to school at least half the time the school was open.

DOWNHAM MARKET GAZETTE November 29th 1879

At the Petty Sessions held at Diss on Monday last, two adult witnesses positively swore that they did not know what month in the year Christmas fell on, and the reason assigned by one of them was 'I am no scholar.'

NORFOLK NEWS January 18th 1845

HALESWORTH — *We have the greatest pleasure in announcing that a plan is to be put in operation for the good of the 'navvies' employed on the East Suffolk Railway, in this town and neighbourhood, which*

we trust will be attended with beneficial results. The Town Hall has been appropriated to the use of the men as a reading room open every evening from half-past seven till nine, where a library and various publications will be provided. This room, it is stated, will be under the management of the active and energetic Scripture Reader who is present to keep order and to instruct in Reading &c. should any of the men desire it.

BECCLES MONTHLY ADVERTISER March 2nd 1857

Somehow self-improvement was seen as more important for men, especially among the working classes. Under the DEBENHAM heading. the FRAMLINGHAM WEEKLY NEWS of December 31st 1864, announced:

Since our last Annual General Meeting, chess and draughts have been purchased for the Reading Room. The game of chess as we [Gentlemen] all know is a very fine game and introduces us into the highest ranks of society; for here we sit down to play with kings and queens, knights and bishops. For the benefit of our lady members, we will endeavour to explain the game of draughts.

Alcohol abuse was one of the main problems of the eighteenth and nineteenth centuries.

What was described as a 'strong water shop' was lately opened in Southwark with this inscription on the sign . . .
Drunk for a penny
Dead drunk for two pence
Clean straw for nothing.

SUFFOLK GAZETTE February 28th 1736

The SUFFOLK CHRONICLE for May 24th 1823, under the heading 'The Pyramid of Drink', described the levels of intoxication caused by the effects of alcohol. These read as follows: '*Sober, comfortable, lively, fresh, very fresh, tipsey, very tipsey, drunk, very drunk, stupidly drunk, dead drunk.*'

INQUEST —*John Clark of Little Whelnetham, in a state of intoxication, fell upon his head when endeavouring to get over a gate and was killed.*

SUFFOLK CHRONICLE June 7th 1817

Mr. Cleveland, landlord at the Anchor Inn, Walberswick, was charged with being drunk, having stripped off his shirt and threatened to fight any man. In his defence he claimed what made him appear drunk was the excitement he experienced from having been obliged to turn a lot of troublesome men from Dunwich out of his house.

Chairman: When do you consider people drunk?

Witness [a lady employee]: *I consider people drunk when they are neither able to walk or talk.*

Chairman: That may be your definition of the term, but it does not agree with ours. Fined 15s inc. costs.

HALESWORTH TIMES July 28th 1857

Any number of inquests used that word *'intoxication'* in their findings, especially road accidents. But there were more light-hearted reports.

DEBENHAM ACCIDENT — *On Friday evening last as Mr. John Mills, in company with four other persons named John Hunt, George Sheldrake, Alfred Holmes and Benjamin Pallant were on their way home from Framlingham where they had been under magisterial inspection, they unfortunately drove against a post, just within the bounds of Debenham. The cart was turned topsy-turvy and the persons above*

Debenham

named were scattered upon the Queen's highway. Fortunately no bones were broken, but their corporeal frames received some unpleasant bruises. We have every reason to believe that if these gentlemen had been teetotallers they would not have been summoned to Framlingham, the cart would not have been turned over, and we should have been spared the painful task of reporting them in the Framlingham Weekly News.

FRAMLINGHAM WEEKLY NEWS February 1st 1868

The growing teetotal movement was seen as a target for light mockery by many local papers.

TEETOTAL TRICK — *Archibald Farquharson of Felzean near Aberdeen was tried for administering to members of a total abstinence soirée, a quantity of laxatives (Jalap and Calomel) in the tea which he had sent with the following note . . . 'From a well-wisher to the health and prosperity of the society.' He pleaded guilty and was fined £10.*

SUFFOLK CHRONICLE September 1840

A TEETOTALLER MADE AN ALE-TASTER — *At the Court Leet held in the Borough of Southwark on Tuesday, a person named Bright objected to serve the office of Ale-taster because he was a teetotaller, but the Recorder, thinking he was on that account better qualified to judge of good ale, and it being stated that he was not obliged to swallow the fluid, he at length consented to take the oath required.*

SUFFOLK CHRONICLE October 10th 1840

WANGFORD — A 'TEETOTAL' LECTURER IN TROUBLE — *On the 10th inst., this village was visited by a young man styling himself a 'Lecturer upon Temperance.' The old school room was engaged for him, and bills were distributed in various parts of the village stating that a Mr. Pegg of London would deliver a lecture that evening in aid of the Temperance Society. A few minutes previous to the doors being opened to the public, the lecturer was presented with a bill from his last lodgings at Southwold, by an officer of police, which he had not the means of paying. It was stated . . . that the pretended teetotaller had been drinking freely at different public houses in the neighbourhood, which he could not* *deny, and the Society being so annoyed at his deception, the doors were closed against him.*

HALESWORTH TIMES August 21st 1860

The vices of the rich were port, brandy and snuff. One local paper came up with a unique calculation.

Every professed, inveterate and incurable snuff-taker, at a moderate computation, takes one pinch every ten minutes. Every pinch, with the agreeable ceremony of blowing and wiping of the nose and other incidental circumstances, consumes a minute and a half. Calculated over a 16 hour day, of 40 snuff-taking years, two years will be dedicated to tickling his nose and two more to blowing it.

LYNN ADVERTISER February 15th 1842

The rich could also indulge themselves in the fashions of the day. Wearing the right things and visiting the right places were very important. The IPSWICH JOURNAL of June 16th 1764 carried an advert for the Bath Houses in Aldeburgh, adding that *'For the conveniency of those who choose bathing in the real ocean, there is a curious machine, that by the assistance of a single person may be run into the sea to any depth proper for bathing.'*

ALDEBURGH — *James Neave respectfully informs the Nobility Gentlemen, Ladies &c. that he has now fitted up WHITE LION INN with very good beds, stables, stands for carriages, and every other requisite accommodation for the convenience of families. Bathing machines, upon the latest and best construction are now ready with careful guides to attend upon them.*

Aldeburgh is a very healthy pleasant sea port, situated at nearly equal distances between Ipswich and Yarmouth, with the advantage of turnpike roads leading to every entrance into the town; the shore dry and even, and well calculated for the conveniency of bathing. The post goes out and in every day; and vessels, for the accommodation of

CROMER URBAN DISTRICT.

BYE-LAWS
AS TO
PUBLIC BATHING

The following are the appointed Stands for Bathing Machines.

No of Stand.	Description or limits of Stand.	Sex to which appropriated.
1	Between the Doctor's Steps Groyne and the Cart Gangway - - - - -	**FEMALE**
2	Between the Doctor's Steps Groyne and a point 100 yards to the East thereof—	
	Before the hour of 8 a.m. daily - -	**MALE**
	After the hour of 8 a.m. daily - -	**MALE & FEMALE**
3	To the East of a point 200 yards to the East of the Doctor's Steps Groyne, being 100 yards East of the Easternmost limit of Stand No. 2 - - - - -	**MALE**
4	To the West of Melbourne House Groyne—	
	Before the hour of 8 a.m. daily - -	**MALE**
	After the hour of 8 a.m. daily - -	**MALE & FEMALE**

GENTLEMEN bathing in the Mixed Bathing Ground must wear a suitable costume, from neck to knee.

Copies of the Bye-laws may be obtained at the Offices of the Council. Persons offending against the Bye-laws are liable to a Penalty of £5.

By Order,

P. E. HANSELL,

Cromer, April, 1898.   *Clerk to the District Council.*

passengers and parcels sail from Dice Quay, London every week. Private
lodgings are numerous and comfortable and all kinds of provisions very
cheap and good.

IPSWICH JOURNAL May 1792

But, given time, even the most genteel of activities could get out
of hand.

Sir, I beg to call the attention of the authorities to what is becoming a
disgraceful custom at this seaside resort.

The bathing at Cromer has been conducted for many years upon a
system, which commends itself to the approval of all who have a respect
for propriety. Perhaps it is not generally known that at the present time,
men are allowed to bathe in the part appropriated to ladies (a man and
his wife being permitted to occupy the same machine) and even women
in that part belonging to gentlemen. Surely this highly indecent state of
things will not be permitted to continue when these facts become known
in the proper quarters. It would soon exclude the better class of visitors,
bring great discredit on all concerned in this matter and render Cromer,
like some foreign places, a vulgar bathing place.

I am, Sir, yours faithfully, A Visitor.
CROMER & NORTH WALSHAM POST August 22nd 1891

From early times, details of what the fashionable person was wearing was required reading, even if only to mock.

Mr. Amelot, minister of the department of Paris, has sent orders to the
Opera not to suffer any women of what distinction soever, to enter that
theatre with feathers or caps that are too high; what occasioned this order
was a Duke being at the opera some time ago, and entirely blinded from
the sight of that performance by the feathers of a lady sitting before him.
The Duke, upon making complaint, obtained the above mentioned order;
several ladies have since been refused admission.

IPSWICH JOURNAL: January 4th 1777

A great man among the Macaronies, who resides in the neighbourhood of
St. James's Street made his appearance on Saturday in the drawing room

in a white cat-skin coat, with buttons about the size of a china saucer, and
with a white muff about two yards and a half in length.

IPSWICH JOURNAL January 25th 1777

IMPORTANT CAUTION — *Ladies who are accustomed to wear*
their dresses extremely low in the back and bosom, or off the shoulders,
are particularly requested to beware of a person, who has for some time
past frequented all places of public amusement and many private par-
ties. He is an elderly gentleman, of venerable appearance and correct
manners; his constant practice, when he observes a lady dressed in the
manner above described, is, with an almost imperceptible and apparently
accidental pressure of a little instrument which he carries in his hand, to
imprint the following words upon her back or shoulders, 'Naked but not
ashamed.' The stain is like that produced by lunar caustic; washing will
not remove it, and it becomes more visible by exposure to the air, so that
nothing but a covering can conceal it. It is said that several ladies were
marked last summer at various places of fashionable resort and that they
cannot, even now, strip for company, without displaying this indelible
badge of disgrace.

SUFFOLK CHRONICLE July 13th 1816

A COMICAL FASHION REPORT — *Eyes continue to be worn, one*
on each side of the nose, and immediately under the brows. There has
been some talk of substituting a single orb of increased size and brilliancy
in the centre of the brow; but after all our achievements in lightning speed,
the world moves slowly, and the idea of a change in the number of eyes
to be worn has not been favourably received, notwithstanding its many
advantages; but the colour is varied to suit the occasion and just now the
prevailing tint is green — a fine sea green. This shade can be best acquired
in Baden-Baden, by continued contemplation of the delicious toilettes of
the demi-monde, but maybe obtained in Paris, Saratoga or on Broadway.
Black, blue, and grey are still worn in the home circle, and are found
very becoming in the nursery, at the family tea table and social evening
gatherings. Noses maintain their position on the centre of the face. The
Grecian or Aquiline is generally preferred but the snubs have held their
position on pretty faces, in defiance of a most determined opposition, and

at present writing are looking up. A very pretty article, of the Grecian type, is now furnished by Goodyear, and it is not improbable that in time all other varieties may disappear. Lips are midway between the nose and the point of the chin, and a pale pink. The coral variety is no longer tolerated, except in girls not yet come out. Teeth will be somewhat larger, and of bluish tint, to correspond with the complexion which must be a dead white and magenta red. Ears are worn, one on each side of the head, with

the hair all carried up so as to give them a peculiar appearance of alert-
ness. There is some prospect of having them pointed, as the mistress of the
grand Duke of D—— has a pet rabbit, which is very much admired in
European court circles.

FRAMLINGHAM WEEKLY NEWS January 11th 1868

Modern safety regulations often seem a bit fussy. However, you
only need to look through nineteenth-century papers to see how
many people died as a result of their clothes catching fire. The
FRAMLINGHAM WEEKLY NEWS for March 20th 1897 reported on

the death of Susannah
Grimwood, who had
gone to wind up the
clock, which stood
on the mantelpiece
of her farmhouse in
Wickham Skeith. In
so doing, the fire had
caught her clothes and
she died later from her
injuries.

The NORFOLK CHRONICLE in January 1842 reported:

A melancholy accident happened at Wortham in Suffolk on Friday last
as Mrs Adams, wife of Mr. Adams, a respectable farmer, was reading by
candlelight. Her head-dress was set on fire, which occasioned her death
on the following day.

These were just two of hundreds of similar cases.

The gulf between rich and poor was accentuated by the system
of service. Even the better-off working class families employed
servants. Those in service were expected to be available all hours
for pitiful wages and to abide by whatever house rules might be
dreamed up by their employers. Clearly there were those who
found there were ways of earning a bit more on the side.

The depravity which is complained of at present, seems not to be confined to the higher orders of society, if we may judge from the following circumstance which lately happened in a tradesman's house in this city:- Being alarmed in the night by the crying of his child, he arose to see what occasioned it, when he found the nurse had left the infant alone: he then proceeded to call his other servant, but found she had also absconded. Repairing to the kitchen and not finding them there, he quietly awaited their arrival in the dark, and had the happiness of hearing one 'faithful' domestic say to the other,

'Is it you?' and the other answer in the affirmative. Then the first told her companion in iniquity that she had made a very profitable excursion, and had got a guinea and a half – the other lamented that she had only got 15s. Upon which the master exclaimed, 'And I have got such information that both of you shall immediately turn out of my house.' And he accordingly compelled them to do so. Surely we need not describe the consternation of the culprits nor caution the public after this to look to the conduct of their servants.

NORFOLK CHRONICLE October 3rd 1807

4
A bit of local colour

The growth of truly local stories in our local papers was a slow process. Initially, it was only the more significant items that got to vie with news from the likes of London and Lisbon.

We hear from Holt that last Saturday, about 3 o'clock in the afternoon, a dismal fire broke out there, which in a little time burnt above eighty houses with the church. It burnt with such vehemency that the shopkeepers in the market place had hardly time to save their books and papers of accounts. The damage the inhabitants sustained by it is modestly computed about £20,000. There is no certain account by what accident this fire happened, nor we do hear that any person was killed by it.
NORWICH POST May 8th 1708

On Sunday the seventh inst. a dreadful fire happened at a place called Badwell Ash, within eight miles of Bury in Suffolk, which consumed almost the whole town, leaving only ten houses standing, whereby 388 families are brought into a deplorable condition, being reduced to the utmost extremity. This unhappy accident was occasioned by two boys that were employed to scare the birds from the fruit &c., and these boys it seems had made a key gun (i.e. the pipe of an old key of a door) with which they intended to fright the birds, but it so happened that one going to call the other on Sunday after dinner, they both strove who should have the gun, upon which one of them having a firebrand in his hand put it to the touch-hole of the gun, which immediately discharged itself, and 'tis supposed the flash, together with the paper that was rammed into it first catch'd hold of the cobwebs, and then of the thatch of the house which kindled such a flame that it could not be extinguished till the whole town was almost laid in ashes. The damage is computed at about 2,000L.

SUFFOLK MERCURY July 15th 1723

Fortunately, more trivial items crept in, and it is these that really give our local papers their individuality.

NORWICH — *We hear that last week, the house of an old widow at Barnham Broom was broke up and robbed by a single man who came to her stark naked to prevent his being known, but the old woman knocked him down with a pewter chamber pot.*

IPSWICH GAZETTE
November 2nd 1734

Barnham Broom

BILDESTON – A SWEET ACCIDENT – *On Thursday evening, an accident occurred here through the carelessness of a common carrier in unloading a cask of treacle weighing between 6 and 7 cwt., belonging to Mr. Osborne, shopkeeper, by which means one of its heads came out, and the whole of the treacle quickly followed. The children of the town, thinking with the sailor, that it was an ill wind that blew no one any good, quickly hastened to the spot, and were soon as busy as cats in a dairy. Some with large pieces of bread commenced dipping, regardless of any dirt that might be intermixed with it, others with mugs and basins, when, as soon as they were filled, an unlucky stone from the opposite side made its way with arrow-like precision and broke them to atoms. Such losses were corrected upon the nearest customer by a handful of the sweet liquid*

Bildeston

being bedaubed in his face, and as quickly returned by the other, until a
great number presented the appearance of Red Indians, their ridiculous
appearance causing the bystanders to forget the heavy loss that must nec-
essarily fall upon someone, and heartily joining the loud laugh, whilst
they each formed a striking contrast to the worthy shopkeeper, whose
countenance could only be faithfully portrayed by George Cruickshank.
SUFFOLK CHRONICLE August 5th 1848

CHARSFIELD – ADVENTURE WITH A TRACTION ENGINE
– On Saturday afternoon, about 3 o'clock, a traction engine, with straw
pitcher and drum was proceeding down the back road, Charsfield, when
in order to allow another vehicle to pass, it drew to the side of the road,
when the wheels of the engine skidded, with the result that the ponderous
engine precipitated into the ditch. All the king's horses and all the king's
men could not get it out again on the Saturday, and so it was left. Efforts
were again made on Sunday, with a successful result. About 200 inhabit-
ants of the village congregated and were quite excited at the efforts.
WOODBRIDGE REPORTER December 11th 1902

HALSTEAD — *The Halstead town crier was sent round on Saturday last to cry the price of meat for a weaver who has recently taken up the trade of a butcher. He cried the following rhyme.*

> *At sixpence per pound, don't be mistaken,*
> *Beef can be had of Joseph Bacon;*
> *Mutton at sevenpence, which is prime,*
> *And steaks at eightpence, by this time;*
> *So when you want to buy some meat,*
> *'Tis near the White Horse, Parsonage Street.*

This announcement caused roars of laughter and generated enormous interest in the cheap meat, so the butcher practically sold out.

SUFFOLK AND ESSEX FREE PRESS May 3rd 1866

LINES BY AN IDIOT IN A COLCHESTER ASYLUM

I hear that at Bury, you've got a bazaar
To supply us with water in pipes from afar.
Well! Water is good, we are all quite aware,
But we hold that mild beer is far better fare.
Now we know that at Bury for years there has been
An excellent brewery, by name that of Greene;
So we fervently pray if you wish us good cheer
That instead of the water, you'd send us the beer;
And since we've no brains, we need hardly to dread
Any evil effects if it gets to our head.

BURY POST around 1870

As some boys were lately playing near a windmill at Westerfield, one of them, whose name is Fryett, about nine years old, was caught by the sails and carried round four times, when, being discerned by the miller, he was released from his perilous situation without sustaining any injury.

SUFFOLK CHRONICLE March 6th 1802

ALARMING SNOW AFFRAY — *On Wednesday morning last, the town of Stowmarket was the scene of a tremendous battle carried on by means of snowballs . . . The late heavy and drifted fall of snow having occasioned a complete stagnation of business, (the roads being impass-*

able) the young men connected with two of the principal shops in the town, deserted the counter and being equal in number, five on each side, repaired to the market place as a suitable spot to carry on their operations . . . The scene at length became of the most enlivening and animating description, and amusing in the highest degree to the spectators who had by this time congregated in vast numbers . . . Five hats were unroofed, breaches were effected in sundry coats and unmentionables so large and conspicuous as to render them scarcely decent, and though no bones were broken, several windows were fractured. After two hours' contest, both parties were compelled from sheer exhaustion to sound a retreat.

Thus ended this tumult and terrible riot.

And Stowmarket recovered its usual quiet.

SUFFOLK CHRONICLE December 31st 1836

DISS MERE — *This large piece of water containing about eight acres, having been covered over with ice by the seasonable weather of the past week, has been very densely thronged with skaters, sliders, &c. On Monday, members of the Diss Cricket Club played a game or two on its glassy surface. On Tuesday and Wednesday, other parties were seen joining in games of tenpins, heedless of the cold and snow. The lovers of camping,* too, and such like manly games have amused themselves on its surface. We have not heard of any accident, save a cold bath to a few young urchins.*

SUFFOLK CHRONICLE January 20th 1838

*Camping was a violent form of football popular in Suffolk at the time.

The machine from Norwich to St. Edmund's Bury was detained at Botesdale all last Thursday night, the 8th inst., by the inclemency of the weather; and the coachman attempting to go forward next day, it was set fast near Stanton in the snow which was at least ten feet deep. Some of the passengers were obliged to walk to Ixworth and two ladies who were passengers were with great difficulty carried thither on horseback.

IPSWICH JOURNAL January 7th 1767
(this article refers back to a similar bad winter in 1739)

At Lowestoft in March 1846, an unusual auction was reported. A local fisherman, Mr Roberts, had refused to pay a tithe of 10s 3d on his meagre fish catches to Rev. F. Cunningham and the process of law led to the seizure of his furniture. These items were offered at auction.

> *The large room was crowded with persons . . . who maintained a profound silence when the goods were offered for sale . . no sound was heard but the voice of the auctioneer. A dozen times at least he had to ask for a bid, but in vain.*
>
> NORFOLK NEWS

Churchwardens and constables had obtained a magistrate's order to remove 13 chairs and a table. This caused great resentment in the town. Even the NORFOLK NEWS considered the Lowestoft vicar had *'pushed the law to its extremity and that this "Christ's dole" as it was called was originally a voluntary offering to eke out the insufficient stipend of the clergyman'.* It was very clear which man in this case was the wealthier.

It sometimes seems remarkable the extent to which editors of some local papers were prepared to mock individual members of their readership, treading a thin line between investigative journalism and poking their noses into people's private business. These two articles from the SWAFFHAM JOURNAL feature in a column by a reporter glorying in the title 'Will-o'-th'-wisp.'

> *Jones' wife has left him, I learn. I have expected this long since. If short diet, a black eye or so occasionally and an uncomfortable home could conduce in any degree towards conjugal misery, Jones' wife has had her cup to over-flowing. Jones, old friend, you are 'dropped on' at last. Women do turn against their tormentors once in a Queen's reign and you have had a clear ocular demonstration of the truth of it.*
>
> SWAFFHAM JOURNAL November 8th 1879

> *A young man in this town courted the cook at ——. She gave him 2lbs of butter. Unfortunately, the mistress asked after this same butter and she said the cat ate it. The mistress weighed the cat and found it no heavier, so gave the girl a month's notice.*
>
> *The young man referred to is in hot water with his love. She lays all the blame on him and says, 'if it hadn't been for you I would never have*

done such a thing.' This is all very fine, but she did similar tricks when in service at Hunstanton, Dereham &c. You see, I know you, my dear.

SWAFFHAM JOURNAL September 6th 1879

However, comment on local places and events has traditionally been an essential part of local reporting.

LYNN – THE MART – *The attractions this year are much below par. Indeed each year brings it lower in the scale of respectability. Once it was a mart, and valuable goods were regularly exposed for sale by persons who were well known to many of the inhabitants. It is far different now. A few bazaars, a large number of toys and a host of gingerbread stalls, with the usual exhibition of dwarfs or giants, a minor theatre and boxing with drinking booths form the source of attraction to thousands who throng our streets. Most of the trade in the town would gladly dispense with its noise and profitless bustle. On Tuesday, the light-fingered gentry plied their trade with great success. Two parties lost their gold watches and gold chains and sundry purses changed owners with impunity.*

NORFOLK NEWS February 29th 1852

LYNN.

Loads of Delicious Mischief carried from Loads of Mud & Water

There was a great flood in King's Lynn,
When the tide in St. Marg'rets rushed in,
Girls with pretty feet, jump'd up on their seat;
And laughed at the plight they were in.

But the fun was in getting them out,
When the gents all hugged them about;
The laughing and mockings at their pretty stockings
Would have cured anyone of the gout.

HUNSTANTON TELEPHONE March 16th 1883

By way of explanation regarding their mistrust of these *'itinerant vendors,'* the Lynn Advertiser for March 1st 1843 described the trick played by a cheese-seller. *'Plugged cheeses were exhibited where plugs of superior cheese were inserted, from which the purchaser was invited to taste, unaware that the rest tasted of boiled peas or rancid lard.'*

HUNSTANTON TELEPHONE March 16th 1883

A man named DEATH cut his throat at Norwich a few days ago and then went to the Norfolk & Norwich Hospital to have it sewed up. He is almost himself again.

DISS EXPRESS March 16th 1866

Advertising plays a key part in our understanding of the past. The items for sale and how they were offered speak volumes about the way our ancestors lived.

A very nicely got up and useful office calendar for the present year has been issued by Messrs. Jarrold & Sons. It is admirably suited to a counting house or office, or even private house, being artistically printed in pretty colours.

YARMOUTH INDEPENDENT January 20th 1894

This is not too different from what we might read now, except a calendar today would probably appear for sale the previous September.

Let us now look at the two cathedral towns covered by this book and articles relating to those very buildings. In October 1893, the EASTERN DAILY PRESS drew people's attention to *'the perilous condition of Norwich Cathedral'*. Apparently, investigations had revealed *'woodwork including rafters is rotten, many windows are in a dilapidated state, stone-work is crumbling and falling out; wet having got into the walls is making them bulge'*. A restoration fund was opened immediately.

A hundred years earlier, behind the Cathedral at Bury, a strange discovery was being made.

Some workmen who were employed in the ruins of the Abbey digging for stone found a leaden coffin, made after the ancient custom, exactly the

shape of the body. This had been enclosed in an oak case, which by length of time was decayed, but the lead remained quite perfect. On searching it close, it was found to be the body of Thomas Beaufort, Duke of Exeter, Uncle to Henry the Fifth, and deposited here in 1427. The workmen opened the lead and, to their surprise, found the flesh, hair and toe and handnails as perfect and found as though he had not been dead six hours. The corpse was done up in a pickle and the head and face wrapped up in sear cloth. A surgeon in the neighbourhood was sent for who made an incision on the breast and declares the flesh cut as firm as a living subject and there was even an appearance of blood. Multitudes of people were present and saw the same. At the time, the corpse was not in the least noisome, but being exposed to the air, it presently became putrid and offensive. The workmen coming early on Friday morning resolved to make prize of the lead, and therefore cut him out, tumbled him into a hole near at hand and threw the dirt on him. The lead was conveyed directly to a plumbers and there sold for twenty-two shillings. Thus in Shakespeare's phrase was a great man knocked about the sconce with a dirty shovel.

NORWICH MERCURY February 29th 1792

BUMPING — *On Monday last a ludicrously serious fracas took place at Woodbridge arising out of one of those venerable and time-honoured customs . . . It was the day set apart for perambulating the boundaries of the parish, and inhabitants stationed themselves on the market hill for the accommodation of youngsters, strangers and others who might* *be unacquainted with the exact extent of the parish. An officer of the 54th attempted to break through the discipline of the day; and it was not until after a severe struggle that numerical superiority compelled him to submit to have . . . several honourable bumps against a post on the hill. The news of this dire event no sooner reached the barracks than a party of Irish soldiers, burning with anger at the supposed indignity which had been shewn to their officer rushed down the hill with their characteristic alacrity. Giving a flourish with their shillelaghs, they bade defiance to the populace. A conflict instantly ensued, and in a few moments, the lads of St. Patrick exchanging thumps for bumps completely cleared the hill and marched off in triumph.*

SUFFOLK CHRONICLE May 29th 1813

5

Crime and punishment

He who takes what isn't his'n
When he's cotched is sent to pris'n

SWAFFHAM JOURNAL March 1st 1879

From the word go, newspaper editors latched on to the idea that their readership enjoyed reading about the dreadful things that those on the fringes of society might get up to. Many of these 'crimes' seem trivial by today's standards, or in some cases hardly crimes at all. Take for example, the case of Caroline Jefferies of Leiston, who pleaded guilty to stealing one onion, to the value of 2*d*, and was fined, with costs, 18 shillings (FRAMLINGHAM WEEKLY NEWS May 23rd 1868).

Also,

Yesterday John Whitehead and John Harrison were taken up and committed to gaol for the space of one month, to hard labour, for singing of seditious ballads and being dressed in a ridiculous manner with paper stars and garters, and horns tipped with gold in their hats, and for being loose, idle and disorderly persons, not having any visible way of living.

IPSWICH JOURNAL February 4th 1744

Samuel Chenery, servant of Mr. G. Ruffle of Lavenham, was on Wednesday last convicted in the mitigated penalty of 5s. for riding on the shafts of his master's wagon with the horses on full trot on the King's highway in the parish of Gt. Waldingfield.

Suffolk Chronicle February 10th 1816

This was one of dozens of such cases.

Another common problem of the horse-drawn age was 'furious driving'. The high number of road accidents, a number being fatal, led to a determination to deal with such an outrage. In February 1816, according to the Suffolk Chronicle, *John Copping and John Hammond, servants of Mr. Geo. Simpson of Stonham Aspall, were convicted and fined 10s. each for driving their master's wagons furiously upon the King's highway'.* Later, in July 1827, J. Cato and R. Bean were sentenced to transportation for the same crime.

Ralph Garrett of Great Easton and M. Yewlett of Finchingfield were fined £1.10s. each at Dunmow petty sessions for travelling on a Sunday. The Magistrates declared it was their intention to put down Sunday travelling in their district.

Bury and Norwich Post February 3rd 1839

Mr. Limmer, baker of Stowmarket, was charged with riding in a 2nd class carriage from Haughley to Stowmarket, having only a 3rd class ticket.

WEST SUFFOLK AND N. ESSEX FREE PRESS: May 29th 1856

Elizabeth Pryke of Wickham Skeith, single woman, was convicted of being a disorderly person and lewd woman having greatly increased the burden of this parish by having five bastard children in four births. She was sentenced to twelve months imprisonment.

Peter O'Brien was convicted as a rogue and vagabond for begging in the parish of Ramsholt, and pretending to have been struck by lightning. He was given three months hard labour.

BURY GAZETTE July 28th 1824

HALESWORTH PETTY SESSIONS — *John Leggett, 12, a tramp, pleaded guilty to stealing one brass caster, the property of John Andrews of Wangford. One month's imprisonment, followed by Reformatory 4 years.*

HALESWORTH TIMES November 17th 1857

James Hughes of Ipswich pleaded guilty to wantonly ringing the doorbell of Mrs. Pritty and running away. He was fined 1s. and 4s. costs.

IPSWICH AND COLCHESTER TIMES December 10th 1858

William Cator, a hawker of sweets, was charged with placing his stall against the footpath to the annoyance of passers-by.

YARMOUTH INDEPENDENT January 1863

DRUNK AND RIOTOUS – *William Woolnough, postmaster at Blaxhall was charged with being drunk and disorderly on the 9th inst. Police Constables Simons and Clarke gave evidence to the effect that the defendant was in the street in Blaxhall, near midnight, partly stripped, with his braces hanging down. He was very drunk and used bad language. They had great trouble in getting him home. He was fined 6s, with 17s 6d costs.*

FRAMLINGHAM WEEKLY NEWS May 23rd 1868

A lad named Collins, charged with throwing a potato at the head of Mr. J. Adcock in Middlegate on Sunday was cautioned and ordered to pay costs of 6s 6d.

NORTH NORFOLK AND YARMOUTH CONSTITUTIONALIST
January 13th 1872

As time progressed, more space was given to crime – its description, detection and its final outcome. In the nineteenth century, every week would produce court reports from the Assizes, Quarter Sessions, Borough Courts and Petty Sessions throughout the county as well as juicy titbits from elsewhere.

Poaching, its prevention and its effects all featured regularly in the local press.

HADLEIGH – *Whereas divers idle and unqualified persons, to the shameful neglect of their proper and lawful employments have of late taken, killed and destroyed the GAME and FISH within the manor of Hadleigh Hall; this therefore is to give notice that any such persons detected in having, taking or killing any hare, pheasant, partridge or any game whatsoever, or of keeping or using any greyhounds, setting-dogs, lurchers, Hays,*

Guns or other engines within the said manor for the killing or destroying of the game . . . will be prosecuted according to the law.

IPSWICH JOURNAL November 1st 1774

A few days since, as the Rev. Mr. Lawson, Curate of Needham Market, a respectable clergyman 62 years of age, was walking and leisurely botanizing near the plantations on Barking Hall, he was caught in a man-trap, and though some persons were attracted to the spot by his cries, they were unable to release him, and he remained for nearly an hour and a

half, suffering under the most excruciating pain, before the gamekeeper could be found to unlock this worthy gentleman, whose leg was found to be very much lacerated, but we are happy to hear, not dangerously.

SUFFOLK CHRONICLE January 20th 1816

On Monday last an unfortunate accident occurred to the three sons of Admiral Wilson, near Redgrave in this county. The three young gentlemen, whilst out shooting, entered a preserve, when one of their dogs touched the wire of a spring gun, and all were much wounded by its contents. One of the young gentlemen was shot in the head and is in a very precarious situation. Another was wounded in the stomach and one through the hand.

SUFFOLK CHRONICLE January 19th 1822

A few days ago, the gamekeeper of R.Pettiward Esq. [at Great Finborough, near Stowmarket] *had a narrow escape from a spring-gun which had been placed by poachers where they expected him to walk. Such an act will doubtless be characterised as diabolical. It was a deliberate purpose of murdering or maiming.*

BURY & NORWICH POST January 4th 1826

GAME TRESPASS — *Harry Beck of Charsfield and Robert Smith of the same parish were charged by Arthur Stanway, gamekeeper to his Grace the Duke of Hamilton, with trespassing in search of game . . .*

George Murton, gamekeeper, said he heard a gun fired and went to the spot and saw the two defendants looking about. There was a gun lying on the bank and some partridges flew up. Defendants said they had done nothing wrong, and offered to treat witness with two pints of gin and beer, which he declined and said, 'I have got you at last.' They were convicted and fined 5s. and 12s. costs each.

WOODBRIDGE REPORTER January 26th 1881

Poachers could be highly organised, and in a case reported by the NORFOLK NEWS in February 1852, '*a formidable gang*' were taken at Thetford. Thomas Bantick, Jeffrey Reeve and Charles Hustler of Ixworth in Suffolk were arrested along with Ben Knights, described as their banker and a man by the name of Thacker, known locally as a receiver and distributor of illegally taken game.

Whilst it thoroughly irritated the landowners, poaching was only regarded as a misdemeanour in legal terms, unless it carried with it acts of violence against the keepers. A typical case was one reported in the EASTERN DAILY PRESS in January 1896, when '*a couple of armed men around Briston Common, named Wylie and Rudd, tolerably well-known to our readers, were apprehended after 12 constables joined in the hue and cry*'. Evidence was collected, including prints of their shoes. However, bringing them to trial was made all the more difficult by the determination of most of the labouring community to protect the poachers.

Labourers in the locality defend them and baulk the endeavours of the police. As one said of gamekeepers, 'when they hear the guns go off, why don't the b——s keep at home?' Around Briston and Edgefield, a successful night's poaching means drinks all round, which accounts for the popularity of the poachers.

In this case, keepers had been shot at, leaving one seriously injured. The landowner determined to rid his land of poachers was Lord Hastings. A generation earlier, the same estate had been the focus of a wonderful poaching tale.

In the NORFOLK NEWS of February 12th 1853, readers were told of the indictment of Rev. Arthur Francis Sheppard, curate of Little Snoring and East Barsham, for poaching. At the trial, the evidence presented was so muddled and incomprehensible, the case was dismissed, but it didn't end there. There had been a series of acrimonious letters passed between Lord Hastings and Mr Sheppard, which finally the exasperated curate sent to the press. And they published them in full. Here are just the first two.

SIR — My keeper has just informed me you have been hunting my plantation with your dog. I have ordered him to proceed against you. I am only sorry to say you have been very guilty of very disgraceful conduct as a gentleman, and I can only add that I regret that you have got a black coat. I have given my keeper orders to prevent your passing over my lands between Barsham and Snoring; you shall not put your foot in any part of my property. I have directed him not to receive any insolent language from your mouth. If you do so, I trust he will give you that which you have long deserved, a good thrashing.

Sir, I remain your obedient servant,

HASTINGS

To which Sheppard replied:

My Lord — I had doubts whether I should condescend to notice your most extraordinary epistle, but . . .

. . . which is probably enough to indicate the nature of what was a long and entertaining dialogue that became increasingly heated, whilst still conducted with an air of grudging politeness.

THE HEIGHT OF IMPUDENCE — *On the night of Monday 23rd [Nov] the premises of Mr. Armstrong, Eastgate St., Bury St. Edmunds were entered and a pair of ducks stolen therefrom. On Thursday morning, the skin of a rabbit was found on the premises, with the following note tied between its ears:*

> *'sir i am very much oblige to you for the 2 Ducks And Rabit i shall come after the Pig a week before Christmas. Pleas to fat all your fowls and Rabbits for the Ducks Was very good but the Rabbit was tough.'*

The rabbit was not missed until the skin was found, and there can be no doubt but that it was stolen when the ducks were.

HALESWORTH TIMES November 28th 1857

On the night of the 1st inst., twelve poachers were firing at pheasants in the woods of Mr. Lane of Barningham. After they had killed as many as they thought proper, they drew up before his house, played several tunes on the German Flute, fired a volley, wished Mr. Lane a good morning, gave three cheers and then retired.

NORFOLK CHRONICLE December 1785

And so to highwaymen. The SUFFOLK GAZETTE of October 11th 1735 reported one of the many exploits of the celebrated highwayman Dick Turpin. Here, Turpin, Rowden and his gang robbed a farmer of four pounds and turned his horse loose, before moving on to rob two further gentlemen of a watch and some money. On this occasion, no violence appears to have been used.

The roads out of London provided easy pickings for the highwaymen of the mid-18th century. The IPSWICH JOURNAL of October 29th 1743 carried reports of a number of highway robberies including three highwaymen who robbed upwards of 50

persons in coaches (including the Colchester stagecoach) attacking and disappearing on horseback, without any opposition.

On Monday last, a wholesale butcher was robb'd in a very gallant manner near Rumford in Essex. The affair was as follows: he was attack'd at first by a woman, mounted on a very good horse with a side-saddle &c. She presented a pistol at him and demanded his money; he was amaz'd at such a behaviour in one of her sex, and told her he did not understand what she meant. By this time, a gentleman of her acquaintance came up and told him he was a brute to make any hesitation in granting what a lady requested of him, and swore D—n his B—d if he did not immediately gratify her desire, he would shoot him thro' the head. At the sight of the gentleman's pistol, the butcher thought proper to grant the lady six guineas, some silver and his watch; which done; they parted in a most compliant manner.

IPSWICH GAZETTE November 29th 1735

Friday morning a Northern sportsman, having finished his negotiations at Newmarket, was met on his road to the North, on the hill between the Rubbing-house and Bottisham, by a single highwayman who presented a pistol to his breast and demanded his money; but upon being told the truth, that a bad run had taken it all from him, the highwayman gener-

ously gave him a guinea to bear his losses, an instance of compassion seldom to be met with amongst his brother sportsmen.

IPSWICH JOURNAL June 2nd 1764

On Tuesday last, at about 8 o'clock at night, as Mr. Sayer, miller of Rumburgh, was returning home on foot from Halesworth Market, two fellows rushed upon him at a lonely spot in the parish of Wissett, knocked him down with bludgeons and robbed him of two five pound notes and three sovereigns, leaving him in an insensible state from their brutal usage.

IPSWICH JOURNAL February 10th 1844

Of course, the highwayman did not always come off best. In the NORWICH MERCURY of September 17th 1774, readers were told of an attempted robbery near Cambridge where the felon was shot in the forehead by the guard armed with a blunderbuss. The man quickly died from his injuries. *'He had no firearms about him, but made use of a candlestick instead of a pistol.'* More fortunate was the 'gentleman of the road' reported in the NORWICH MERCURY in January 1762. Having stopped the Norwich coach in Epping Forest, *'he informed the company he was very poor; a little money would at that time be particularly useful; whereupon they collected six guineas, with which he rode off well satisfied'.*

Highway robbery was still going on in May 1890. The STOWMARKET COURIER reported the case of Robert Snell of Raingate Street, Bury, who was robbed of 11s by a thief who knocked him down and took his money on the road from Beyton to Bury.

Smuggling has always been a favourite activity of East Anglian residents, as these following stories show.

On Monday, one Robert Caston, who was formerly committed to our gaol for robbing the Custom House, but made his escape and stole a fishing boat in the river, which he carried away and sold at Calais, was by the diligence of some Constables, retaken and recommitted, and it is hoped he will now meet with his deserts.

SUFFOLK GAZETTE December 20th 1735

Thursday, at a sale at the excise office of smuggled teas, the most ordinary teas were sold for upwards of 7s. a pound.

SUFFOLK GAZETTE July 31st 1736

On Wednesday, Mr. Boldra, officer of the Customs, with the assistance of five dragoons of the Iniskilling Regiment, seized in a vault under Lowestoft cliff sixteen half-ankers of geneva and thirteen bags of tea, which he conveyed to the port of Yarmouth.

IPSWICH JOURNAL November 11th 1769

A smuggling cutter was brought into Harwich having on board a large quantity of spirits and 6,720lbs of tea. It is intended in future to burn these goods instead of selling them as smugglers are in the habit of re-buying them at a low rate.

IPSWICH JOURNAL October 2nd 1784

On Thursday last, near seven hundred pound weight of human hair, which had been smuggled from France, was seiz'd on the Kent Road by some customhouse officers.

IPSWICH JOURNAL August 1st 1752

This week nearly fifty barbers have been convicted of using flour in their trade and fined in the penalty of 20L each.

IPSWICH JOURNAL August 1st 1752

This refers to the fact that wig-powder was highly taxed, and barbers were in the habit of adulterating it with flour to make it go further (with disastrous effects if rained upon).

Wednesday last, a seizure was made on Hollesley beach (by William Wood, sitter of his Majesty's boat at Bawdsey ferry, in the port of Woodbridge, with an Officer of Excise, assisted by a party of the 3rd Regiment of Dragoon Guards) of about 500 gallons of Geneva and 60 gallons of Brandy, all of which were lodged at Woodbridge. One of the Dragoons, being left in charge with a part of the above seizure, got intoxicated and died in consequence.

SUFFOLK CHRONICLE December 12th 1801

Certain parts of the coast became infamous as landing points for smuggled goods. This picture looks South from Dunwich, towards the notorious 'Sizewell gap.'

Smuggling was the organised crime of its day and could be a violent business:

NEEDHAM MARKET — *We are credibly informed that about five weeks since, a quantity of tea was secreted in a barn at Onehouse near Stowmarket by some smugglers; on their return in order to carry the tea away, missing three bags, they imagined that a labourer of Onehouse aforesaid, had stolen them and in order to make the poor man confess, tied him to post in a wood called Northfield Wood, held him upon a tree and beat him in a very cruel manner, although the poor man protested that he was entirely innocent of the charge.*

IPSWICH JOURNAL March 22nd 1777

In February 1870, the STOWMARKET COURIER described a case of smuggling where carcases of dead pigs, arriving by ship in Harwich, were stuffed with tobacco. Of course, you couldn't always rely on the authenticity or purity of the smuggled goods you bought. The NORWICH GAZETTE in February 1726 described the seizure of *'a great quantity of oak leaves mixed with tobacco and sloe-leaves designed for tea . . . which were burnt on Tower Hill'.* The NORWICH,

Old Harwich

YARMOUTH & LYNN COURIER in October 1818 gave details of a consignment of smuggled tea *'of a lively blue colour which was analysed and found to contain copper'.*

When John Carbold (35), John Doe (26) and Charles Gawen (37) hanged at Tyburn, having been taken for smuggling near Norwich in 1750, detailed accounts of their lives were published in the NORWICH MERCURY. Clearly they were the token three to be executed from a large group of Yarmouth smugglers; Gawen's story sounds particularly pathetic.

> *CHARLES GAWEN, aged 37, was born within three miles of Beccles and was bred a shoemaker in the town. About 7 years after his time was out, he took to the sea and was owner of boats and keels, which he worked in himself for some time before he became a smuggler. But he has followed that trade a few years, he says, with success, and whatever business he was concerned in was done without any interruption. He said of himself that he never was given to quarrelling or committing any outrages . . . He was nicknamed 'The Papist' from the dark cast of his countenance, which bore no small resemblance to the complexion of the people on the continent of France and Spain, but was bred a protestant and so declared to die. His behaviour in Newgate was uncommonly sober and quiet from first to last and from the time of conviction appeared with the utmost resignation to the will of God and his sentence. If being a smuggler means death, he said he had his due, but he forgave as he hoped to be forgiven and professed to have hopes in another life through the merits of Christ that he should be happy.*
>
> NORWICH MERCURY April 7th 1750

For sea-based crime, this was hard to beat:

> **YARMOUTH** — *For alleged piracy in the North Sea . . . John Robert Ross, Albert Chalk & William Preston, masters of local fishing smacks, were accused and remanded. Several fishermen belonging to the smacks were examined, and deposed to going with the prisoners on board the German cutter Deidrich on July 29th last and taking away to their own vessels large quantities of spirits, cigars and scents. It was admitted that*

Yarmouth Quay

the store-room of the cutter was entered . . . and Rule Britannia sung therein, after a bottle of rum had been opened and drunk.
EAST SUFFOLK GAZETTE January 13th 1885

In dealing with crime, punishment meted out by the legal authorities was often harsh, and believed to serve the public's requirements if not those of the offender.

The IPSWICH JOURNAL for August 18th 1744 described the sentence handed out at Guildford to a pair of beggars. They had entered several towns dressed as farmers, pretending their farms had burned down, and asking for help. None of this was true and as a result they were whipped from the town's end to the gallows at Guildford, twice round the market place at Kingston, a similar treatment at Croydon and once again from their prison to the Bear at the Bridge foot and back again to gaol. After that they were to continue to serve 6 months' hard labour, and afterwards to be *'sent for soldiers into America'.*

The treatment of female felons was to become quite an issue.

One Anne Butler, alias Cossey Nan, a notorious old offender, who has been several times whipt, was convicted of felony and ordered to be

whipt this day, 2 lashes under every sign from the Hall to the Star in the market and back again.

NORWICH MERCURY July 20th 1751

We hear that one Elizabeth Peckard was tried for wilfully and maliciously poisoning her husband, and was ordered to be burnt [alive]. The surgeon who examined the husband's body deposed that he found, on searching, arsenic sufficient for poisoning 1000 persons.

NORWICH MERCURY April 7th 1750

Emma Polyqueska was brought up on remand for attempting to commit suicide by throwing herself into the river. The magistrates discharged the prisoner, stating that as she had been imprisoned for a week, it would act as a caution to her.

DOWNHAM MARKET GAZETTE December 6th 1879

In an open letter (published by the NORFOLK CHRONICLE) to the reformer William Wilberforce, an anonymous barrister in 1786 spoke of public whipping *'tending to destroy the finest sensations of delicacy natural to a woman . . . stripping her and tying her naked to a post in a public street, to say nothing of the lash of the executioner*. It would still be some years before such practices were eradicated.

The SUFFOLK CHRONICLE for March 28th 1835 reported a case from the Cambridgeshire Assizes in which John Bond of Bassingbourne was indicted for the wilful murder of his wife by beating her with a cod-fish, which she had refused to cook for him as he had arrived home late and she was in the advanced stages of pregnancy. He was found guilty of manslaughter and transported to Australia for life.

Just about all of our local papers before 1850 were weekly. Often the first reference to a crime being committed would be a reward notice, but as clear-up rates were quite good, it would often be published alongside an account of the arrest, as was the case described in this advertisement in the IPSWICH JOURNAL of November 10th 1759:

LITTLE GLEMHAM, Suffolk, Nov. 8, 1759.

Whereas the Shop of Mrs. GRACE ABLETT of this Town was broke open on MONDAY the 5th Inftant, and robbed by Perfon or Perfons unknown of feveral Sorts of Goods, viz.

One Piece of Lomb Dowlas, containing 30 Yards; one ditto of Wafh ditto, 30 Yards; one ditto of black ground Cotton, 14 Yards; five Yards and 1-qr. of ftriped Cotton, flowered; three or four Dozen of yard-wide Silk Handkerchiefs of different Patterns; two or three Dozen of South-Sea ditto; one Piece of Thickfet, containing feven or eight Yards; one Dozen Women's red Worfted Stockings; 11 Pair of Men's white ribb'd ditto; and feveral other Goods to a confiderable Value.

Whoever will apprehend, or caufe to be apprehended, one or more of them, fo that he, fhe, or they, may be brought to Juftice and convicted, fhall have TEN GUINEAS Reward; and if any one or more of them will difcover their Accomplice or Accomplices, that he, fhe, or they, be convicted as aforefaid, they fhall have the Sum of TEN GUINEAS.   GRACE ABLETT.

This advert had been paid for, so was printed although it was irrelevant by the time the paper came out, as will be seen from the news report published in the same issue of the paper and reproduced overleaf.

On Monday Benj. Buck of Athelington, Labourer, was committed to the County Gaol in this Town, by the Rev. Mr. Ph. Carter, being charged on Oath with breaking open the Shop of Mrs. Grace Ablett of Little Glemham, on Monday the 5th Inftant, in the Night, and ftealing from thence feveral Parcels of Drapery and Mercery Goods.—See an Advertifement in our laft, defcribing Part of the Goods miffing.

The next Day Tho. Buck, a Tanner in Framlingham, Brother to the above-mentioned Benj. Buck, was committed to the fame Goal by Michael Thirkle, Efq; on his own Confeffion that he had been jointly concerned with his Brother in robbing Mrs. Ablett. Part of the Goods are found, and owned by Tho. Buck to have been ftolen from her; and Yefterday Benj. Buck confeffed that he and his Brother committed the faid Robbery.

It being fufpected, that they had been guilty of other Offences, particularly fome lately committed near Beccles, Bungay and Harlefton, they were both of them examined on thefe Points; and Tho. Buck declared, that his Brother had told him, that, foon after laft Harveft, he broke into the Houfe of a Widow at Mettingham near Bungay (he thinks her Name is Crofs), and ftole fome Silver Spoons and a Cotton Gown; which Gown he fold to a near Relation whom he named; fo that, we fuppofe, it may be feen by the Perfon who loft it.

We are informed that the faid Benj. Buck has been a Prifoner in this Goal two or three Times before, for Crimes of the like Nature. He is about five Foot fix Inches high, about Twenty-five Years of Age, is a fquare-fet Man, with a round Face and frefh Complexion, wears his own brown Hair, has a Scar over his left Eye, and a Lamenefs in his right Thigh.

Of course, most of those indicted for crimes were from the poorest classes. Whilst a bit of money could help to ease your woes should you be convicted, it did not always have the desired effect. Legendary thief-taker and receiver Jonathan Wild finally met his come-uppance in May 1725 at Tyburn. Rather than face his last journey in the ignominious 'cart', he offered to pay 100 guineas to travel to his execution in a coach. According to the NORWICH

Jonathan Wild addressing the crowd before his execution

GAZETTE, the offer was rejected. We were also told that Wild's wife, at his demise, tried to kill herself. She had already seen one husband hanged there.

When, two years later, John Ward Esq. MP was put in the pillory for certain financial irregularities, this was how it was reported:

There was such a concourse of people as has not been known on that occasion. His prosecutors, the Duke and Duchess of Buckingham, also the Duke of Montague, and divers others of the nobility, and many members of the House of Commons were amongst the spectators, several of whom came prepared for pelting him, but were prevented by the constables, who were very numerous. Three of his servants stood on the pillory all the time to ease his neck as much as possible and to wipe the sweat from his face, and supply him with spirits to smell to, but notwithstanding, when he was taken down, he bled much at the mouth and was for some time speechless and senseless. His spirit, it seems, could not bear being exposed in such an ignominious manner, for preventing, which, we are told, he offered very considerable sums and used all other endeavours possible; the rejecting of which, will let those that trust in their strength see, that neither grandeur or wealth can screen them from the punishment due to vile and perfidious actions.

NORWICH MERCURY February 25th 1727

Just in case we might be tempted to feel sorry for him, this was the man who, amongst other documentation, left this remarkable prayer as testament to his remarkable self-centredness:

O Lord, you know that I have nine houses in the city of London, and that I have recently purchased an estate in Essex. Please keep the two counties of Middlesex and Essex from fires and earthquakes. And, as I have also a mortgage in Hertfordshire, I beg you also to have an eye of compassion on that county, and the rest of the counties you may treat as you like. O Lord, help the banks to meet all their bills and make all debtors good men. Give prosperous voyage and safe return to the ship Mermaid because I have not insured it. And because you said 'The days of the wicked are short', I trust that you will not forget your promise as I will inherit an estate on the death of that worthless young man Sir J. L———. Keep my friends from sinking, preserve me from thieves and house-breakers, and make all my servants so honest and faithful that they may always attend to my interests, and never cheat me out of my property night and day.

The prison population, including those coming up for trial, were largely young, many just children. In reporting the Chelmsford Assize in March 1816, the SUFFOLK CHRONICLE notes that of 80 prisoners for trial, a quarter were under 20. They would still be treated in much the same ways as their adult counterparts. But there were those who believed certain crimes required a quite different form of punishment. The SUFFOLK & ESSEX FREE PRESS described a 13-year-old boy who had been struck blind for blasphemy (divine retribution?). Others preferred conducting their own kind of justice:

SUMMARY PUNISHMENT FOR DELINQUENCY — *The silk-weavers of Sudbury, who have raised a fund for paying the expenses of sending delegates . . . were on Tuesday last alarmed at finding that one of their body, who had been appointed treasurer, had decamped with part of the money; they were quickly on the alert and ascertaining that the person was seen on the London Road, pursuit was immediately made, and the delinquent was taken at Halstead and brought back to Sudbury. The enraged weavers instantly proceeded to the work of punishment; they plunged the unhappy wight into a large tub of swill and grains, and then with a mop, which had been dipped into a certain place, covered him with filth, and in this most wretched and disgusting plight, turned him adrift to be hunted out of town. He was seen stealing away with all his honours thick upon him, to repent of not keeping in mind that honesty is the best policy.*

SUFFOLK CHRONICLE March 21st 1829

Sudbury

Two men went into a public house near Tombland, and being in a room by themselves, were detected in attempting to commit an unnatural crime. One made his escape. The neighbours soon assembled about the door . . . and conducted him to a common pump where they gave him a severe ducking.

NORFOLK CHRONICLE 1773

Norwich

ATTEMPT AT SEDUCTION — *A trial of a novel description of a countryman attempting to seduce a servant girl from the paths of virtue took place at Up-Street, Kent, a few days since, before a jury of villagers, there assembled: when after a most patient investigation of the case, the countryman was found guilty and sentenced to be hanged by the heels to the roof of the room for twenty minutes and to drink four pints of strong onion broth — two pints previously to, and the remaining two during the suspension. The delinquent, on hearing the verdict, endeavoured to make his escape . . . but the honest rustics were not to be frustrated, and immediately carried the same into execution, to the no small amusement of the company present.*

SUFFOLK CHRONICLE December 20th 1817

When John and Sarah Hazell were tried for the murder of the child by his first marriage, Sarah alone was found guilty: he merely served a sentence for helping dispose of the body in the river. On his release,

> *he was surrounded by the mob, who after treating him in a cruel manner, carried him down to Eye Bridge, where they tied a rope about his body and threw him over the bridge into the river.*
>
> NORFOLK CHRONICLE June 1784

Later, he was obliged to take refuge in a neighbouring house.

> *A young man who was paying assiduous court to the wife of a dyer had the misfortune to be caught by the enraged husband, who called his workmen about him and without any ceremony, the gallant-so-gay was plunged into a cauldron prepared for imparting a true-blue dye to various fabrics. In a second, the unfortunate youth had acquired such a tint that he dares not appear in public. His friends implored the dyer to restore the poor fellow to his natural hue, but the pitiless answer was, 'it is impossible. He is a beautiful colour and all I can do for him is to change him to a green or a violet.'*
>
> DISS EXPRESS December 1864

Perhaps in such cases, those administering justice had more faith in their own ability than that of the authorities, for, truth to tell, both the guardians of the law and those they sought to arrest could be surprisingly inept.

> **OFF IN A HURRY** — *A man who has been committed for stealing wheat at Warminster escaped on Saturday week while on his way to Fisherton gaol. The two constables were rather economical and hired one horse between them; they agreed to 'ride and tie.' When they arrived at Burden's Hall, the prisoner refused to walk, complaining of being tired. It was agreed that he should ride the remaining three miles. He had no sooner mounted the horse, than he set off at full gallop and has never since been heard of.*
>
> BURY GAZETTE February 4th 1824

James Brown, on the other hand, in breaking into a beer-house in Glemsford in 1841, cut his hand breaking a window. It had been snowing and he bled all the way home. The account in the BURY & NORWICH POST for 17th March that year describes how he left a perfect trail for the constables to follow. He was transported to Van Diemen's Land for ten years for his carelessness.

There were also serious crimes and gaol breaks, some of the most intrepid kind.

On Sunday night, the counting house of Messrs. Oxley & English, merchants, in Kings Street was broken open and robbed. It appears that the thieves made a sort of battering ram of a deal with which they plied their avocation against the window and the shutters with such force that the bar at length gave way, and they had ingress into the room. They then proceeded to break open all the drawers, and finding the key of the iron safe, they took out about seven or eight pounds worth of silver which they pocketed and decamped.

LYNN ADVERTISER February 15th 1842

On Tuesday one Smith, a notorious offender belonging to Yarmouth who fled from thence a few days ago, was apprehended at Costessey and made his escape by swimming across the river, but being closely pursued was taken and being brought to this city and was by the Right Worshipful the Mayor committed to Bridewell in order to be removed to Yarmouth. Being indulg'd with a chamber to lodge in, about ten o'clock the same evening he effected another escape (in his shirt and without breeches) by bending the iron bars of the windows and dropping into the street. In the fall, he fell on a lamp-post, and beat off the lamp-iron.

NORWICH MERCURY April 23rd 1774

Though murder was far less common, crimes warranting the death penalty were quite plentiful. As can be seen from my book, *Death Recorded*, about a thousand criminals received death sentences in Suffolk during the first 200 years of local papers. Of these, about 170 hanged. It seems likely, from my reading of Norfolk trials, that these figures were exceeded in Norfolk Assize Courts. The following two cases were reported in the same year by the local press.

Sarah Bligh, aged 23, was a domestic servant in Hampstead when she became pregnant. According to the DISS EXPRESS in June 1893, a child's body was found floating in a pit at Holme Hale in Norfolk. The cause of death was a blow to the back of a skull. When questioned, Sarah denied she had ever had a child, but a safety-pin identifiable as belonging to a Hampstead hospital was found in her step-mother's home. She then changed her story and claimed the child had fallen down, so the death was accidental. The jury did not believe her and the judge had no option but to pass sentence of death upon her. He chose to leave off the black cap, indicating he expected she would obtain a respite, which she did. The EASTERN DAILY PRESS informed its readers on July 28th that she would now serve life imprisonment for the crime.

ATTEMPTED MURDER AND SUICIDE IN SUFFOLK — *A shocking case of attempted murder and suicide occurred at Cockfield near Bury St. Edmunds yesterday afternoon about four o'clock. Two labourers, neighbours, named Souter and Crick have, it seems, lived unpleasantly owing to the reported persistent annoyance of Mrs. Crick by Souter. In consequence Souter received notice to quit his dwelling. While in the allotments, Souter twice shot at the woman, whose condition is serious. Souter threatened to shoot some spectators who attempted the rescue of his victim, and then fatally fired at himself by applying a stick to the trigger of the gun.*

EASTERN DAILY PRESS October 10th 1893

Serious crime could result in a variety of outcomes, according to the circumstances.

Katherine Hayes was sentenced to be drawn on a hurdle to Tyburn and there burnt alive for petty-treason.

NORWICH GAZETTE April 30th 1726

(Her actual crime was to murder her husband. Her two male accomplices, Thomas Billins and Thomas Wood, were sentenced to hang, though Wood died in Newgate before the sentence could be carried out.)

In the case of the murder of Thomas Reyner at Worthing in Norfolk by John Capes, a shoemaker, it was revealed he had stabbed his wife's lover with one of his leather knives. The court was more in sympathy and following a verdict of 'Guilty to Manslaughter', Capes was branded and released.

The wife died a week before his trial and her body was buried close to that of her lover.
NORWICH GAZETTE August 4th 1729

Executions were given increasing column space. Some of the more spectacular reports came from London, having been taken

from London papers of the time. When the pirate John Gow was hanged at Execution Dock beside the Thames in June 1725, the report had been written by none other than Daniel Defoe himself. He recounted how the executioner, in attempting to put a speedy end to the suffering of Gow, hung on his legs, causing the rope to break and a part of the structure to collapse. Gow had to mount the scaffold again and be hanged a second time.

Worse was to follow in May the following year, when the NORWICH GAZETTE reported another collapsed scaffold that had led to three deaths and many more injuries.

As well as attending a public hanging, you could 'buy the tee-shirt' in the form of a broadsheet, such as the one offered below.

TRIALS FOR MURDER!!!
AT THE SUFFOLK LENT ASSIZES, 1812.

This Day are published, Price One Shilling,
THE TRIAL of EDMUND THROWER, Blacksmith, late of Carbrook, in Norfolk, for the WILFUL MURDER OF THOS. CARTER, and ELIZ. CARTER *HIS DAUGHTER,* On the 16th day of October, 1793, at Cratfield, in the County of Suffolk; AND ALSO THE TRIAL OF JOHN and ELIZABETH SMITH, *For the WILFUL MURDER of MARY ANN SMITH.* An INFANT, aged Eight Years, Daughter of the said JOHN SMITH by a former Wife, By STARVING and CRUELTY, At COOKLEY, in the County of SUFFOLK. *Before the Hon. Mr. Justice Heath,* At the ASSIZES held at BURY, March 21st, 1812. TAKEN IN COURT BY GEORGE KENT.
Bury St. Edmund's: Printed by Gedge and Barker, and sold by all Booksellers in Suffolk, Norfolk, Essex, and Cambridgeshire; and in London by Axtell and Co. 1, Finch-lane, Cornhill.

In that case, public interest was high. It had taken 19 years to bring Edmund Thrower to justice.

Court proceedings made for good reading. The 'twelve good men and true' called upon to ascertain guilt or innocence were supposed to reflect the society of the time. If so, Norwich must have been a city of shopkeepers. According to the NORWICH GAZETTE, the Grand Jury in October 1728 was composed of 24 grocers, the two sheriffs also being grocers.

In 1849, the judicial system of Norfolk came under the gaze of the whole country as James Blomfield Rush, 'the killer in the fog', was tried for a double murder. Rush had been on increasingly bad terms with his landlord, Isaac Jermy, who lived nearby at Stanfield Hall near Wymondham. In late 1848, disguised in a cloak, a figure

Stanfield Hall

entered the Hall, shooting Jermy and his son dead and leaving his wife and a servant severely wounded. Rush was identified and convicted at the next Assize. Both local and national papers were full of the details, as they were of his execution in April 1849. The jury had taken just six minutes to find him guilty. He was reported as showing great bravado at his hanging, even requesting the hangman to *'put the rope a little higher'* and to take his time. Record numbers were able to attend, as special trains had been laid on to bring spectators in to Norwich for the occasion.

JAMES BLOMFIELD RUSH

6

Medicine and disease

Until well into the nineteenth century, every disease was regarded as life-threatening, and was therefore newsworthy. The more bizarre the complaint, the better the story.

The case of a young lady in Kent, who lately died in the 23rd year of her age, of the dropsy, is very remarkable. She had been tapped for it 155 times, in the whole of which 3720 pints of water had been drawn from her, which is 465 gallons or nearly seven hogsheads and a half. She had a good appetite, was cheerful and could walk a mile or two.

IPSWICH JOURNAL January 15th 1780

A child, who had been ill some time from a complaint in his back, was last week brought to a surgeon in Huddersfield, who discovering something lodged in its shoulder actually extracted a needle from the part affected, which the child's mother recollected having swallowed during her pregnancy.

IPSWICH JOURNAL May 30th 1801

Mr. Chubbe, the evening before his death, was with his doctor and friend, Dr. Frost of Hadleigh, having his pulse felt. He asked how the pulse sounded. The doctor observed with some gravity, that it 'beat like the Dead March.'

SUFFOLK CHRONICLE June 5th 1824

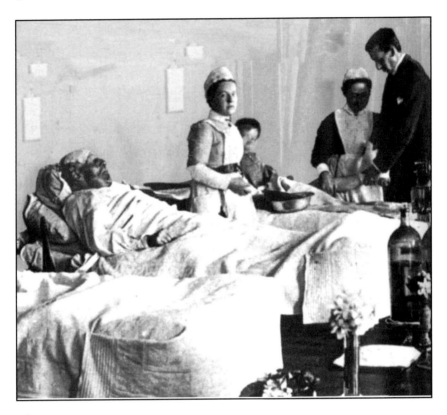

Hospitals in the early 1800s were places to enter with a good deal of trepidation. Even by the end of the century when this picture was taken, they were best avoided and it had become clear that the best way to live comfortably was to seek a healthier way of life.

In August 1882, the THETFORD & WATTON TIMES announced the health-giving properties of Shelfanger Spa near Diss, which *'bids fair to become one of the most popular of baths. I shall be surprised if this health resort does not become one of the most popular in the country.'* The *'hot and cold sea-baths'* of Wivenhoe and Harwich were also announced in similar terms by IPSWICH JOURNALS of the late 1770s. Other watering places included Mundesley (with its commodious bathing machine), Cley, Happisburgh and the Heigham Bathing Place, named Fort George in dedication to the Prince of Wales. It was far from the first health spa in East Anglia.

We hear from Bungay in Suffolk that Mr. King, the apothecary, is now erecting there a COLD BATH which will be finished about Michaelmas and 'tis said that the goodness of the water and the quickness of the spring together with the beautifulness of the situation will render it one of the most useful and pleasant baths in the whole kingdom.

NORWICH GAZETTE September 17th 1726

The same newspaper that summer had reported a number of 'successful' pioneering operations carried out by local surgeons. Mr. John Harmer had carried out 45 operations *'cutting for the stone'* as well as a *'Trepan on a boy with a fracture of the skull where he removed a piece of bone the size of a 6d.'* Mr. Taylor was performing cataract operations, *'restoring sight to those who had been blind for years.'*

In rather the way people today might monitor local traffic problems or the weather, in centuries past, it was helpful to know where not to go in order to stay healthy.

The country people about Cambridge are afraid to go to market on account of the smallpox.

SUFFOLK GAZETTE July 24th 1736

Last week at Oakley in this county, a woman died who about three months since received a bite from a mad dog. She was for a week before she died in extreme agony, but died easy. She was not, however, prevented from biting her husband, who is now under the hands of a skilful apothecary at Diss.

IPSWICH JOURNAL December 10th 1763

Under the heading *'Plague outbreak in Naples – Troops guarding the town'*, the SUFFOLK CHRONICLE (February 10th 1816) reported that whilst a hundred and fifty years had passed since the last outbreak of plague in England, it wasn't very far away. *'The infection is said to have been communicated by the crew of a Turkish vessel wrecked on the Neapolitan coast.'*

Epidemics were bad for business and towns often advertised that they were free from certain prevalent diseases. The following notice was published in all the local papers of the time:

Diss, June 3rd, 1784.

WE, whose Names are under written, do certify That there is not One Person in This Town has the Small-Pox.

Willliam Manning, Minister.

Layman and Norgate
Jno. Darry   } Surgeons.
John Sharman

Benj. Wiseman, jun. } churchwardens.
Zach. Death

In March last, the small-pox broke out in this town; it was of so favourable a kind that the sick did not confine themselves to their houses, by which means the disease was communicated to several families, which induced the inhabitants to submit to a general inoculation. In Eight or Nine days, more than Eleven hundred were inoculated, from the age of One month to between Eighty and Ninety years, of which not One person died. Scarce any of the poor were kept from their labour more than Two or Three days; many not at all. These circumstances are published as inducements to other parishes to adopt the same happy means of eradicating this dreadful disorder.

IPSWICH April 14 — We have great Hopes that this Town will very soon be entirely free from the Small Pox. We have enquir'd of every Physician, Surgeon and Apothecary that we can think of, in the Town, and can hear only of one Person that has the Distemper, which is a Child in St. Hellen's Parish, beyond the Church.

IPSWICH JOURNAL April 1739

It took a long time for many to recognise the fact that the filthy conditions under which people lived were the main cause of much disease.

The YARMOUTH GAZETTE for January 1875 reported that in October and November the previous year, 42 children had died from scarlet fever. They stressed that the disease had, by the time of publication, run its course. An advert appearing in the IPSWICH JOURNAL of March 10th 1767 was designed to discourage Hadleigh people from being inoculated against smallpox. Early forms of inoculation, though usually successful, still left patients as carriers of the disease. The advert emphasised how bringing the disease into the town (at that time free from it) would adversely affect trade and *'sow the infectious seed from one end of the town to the other'.* Principal inhabitants were warned not to go into any pest house within five miles of Hadleigh or to be attended by Mr Bucke, the surgeon. Eleven years later, in June 1778, the IPSWICH JOURNAL announced that the town of Hadleigh was submitting to a general inoculation of the whole population against the disease.

The publishing of cures was widespread, though some sound to us at best doubtful, at worst downright dangerous.

The IPSWICH JOURNAL of May 12th 1764 included adverts for Herring's Norfolk Antidote for the bite of a mad dog, and Tincture of Sage which was supposed to have *'preserved the faculties and memory, warmed the heart, strengthened the stomach and prevented faintness, trembling, and every kind of discomposure'.* Then,

> *The following is said to be an excellent remedy for an asthma: Gum Ammoniac, Venice Soap, Turkey Rhubarb, Russia Castor, fresh green squills, of each two scruples; beat all in a mess and make them into pills of a moderate size. Five taken at night, going to bed, will much relieve the complaint.*
>
> SUFFOLK CHRONICLE December 26th 1801

> *Cure for consumption: in the month of May, gather the flowers from the thorn bush — boil two bunches of the blossoms in half a pint of milk — let it stand till it is about as warm as milk from the cow — drink it first thing in the morning and take a walk immediately afterwards, if the weather is favourable, and a cure will soon be effected.*
>
> IPSWICH JOURNAL May 26th 1827

> *Cure for Lock Jaw — large doses of opium has been shown* [in Chester] *to be a perfect cure for this affliction.*
>
> IPSWICH JOURNAL February 3rd 1827

The SUFFOLK CHRONICLE for April 1822 announced that a vaccination had been developed for 'hooping cough'.

The following advert appeared in the IPSWICH JOURNAL in
March 1791 extolling the virtues of one particular doctor.

HADLEIGH — *The following are some of the many cures performed
by CHRISTIAN KREBS, Surgeon and Oculist, during his six weeks residence at Yarmouth.*

*Charles Lyon, Hatter of Yarmouth, aged above seventy, has been so deaf
that he could not hear the going of a wagon in the street, was restored to
his hearing in a quarter of an hour, that he could hear common conversation, hear the clock and people walk in the street.*

*A daughter of Mary Draper belonging to Yarmouth poor house, has been
afflicted with a Scrophulous Tumour on her head, neck and eyes by which
her sight was nearly lost, cured in three weeks time.*

*A son of Mr. Thomas Brooks, aged about sixteen years, was deaf by an
ulcer in his ear attended with a continual discharge of matter which
smelled very offensive, cured.*

*Thomas Holland, belonging to Yarmouth Poor House, has been blind for
thirteen years so as not to discern an object, can now see a pin.*

*Mrs Sarah Duffy, living on the Church Plain, Yarmouth, has been
afflicted with the rheumatism in her back and loins, so she could not walk
erect, attended with excruciating pains, cured in a short time so that she
walked from Yarmouth to Lowestoft and back with ease.*

*Mr. Edmund Ballett, of Gorleston, aged twenty years, became stone blind
by a violent pain in his head, occasioned by an obstruction in his head
which Mr. Krebs removed in five minutes by his operation by which he
extracted about ten ounces of black matter out of his head, the next day
he could discern colours and the eleventh day after the operation could
read print and writing. Mr. Krebs is to be consulted with at his house at
Hadleigh, Suffolk from nine o'clock in the morning till 1.*

The NORWICH MERCURY for November 23rd 1851 carried adverts
for many elixirs, including

FRAUNCE'S female strengthening pills

BETTON'S true and British oil for preserving the teeth & curing the toothache

MR. JACKSON'S TINCTURE – an effective remedy for the gravel, stone cholick, wind and griping of the guts

STEEL'S SPECIFIC CAKE for the rheumatism

JOHN COLBATH'S anti-apoplectic elixir

DR. RADCLIFF'S specific lozenges for the piles

When a man's back aches it seems to take all the life and energy out of him. Work becomes drudgery, he can't even rest day or night.

The most tastefully served meal fails to tempt his appetite, he finds no pleasure in the company of his family, no pleasure in life at all.

He has tried liniments and plasters, but they haven't cured him. The pain is inside, the plasters and liniments cannot reach it. Yet there *is* a cure—a certain, safe and reliable cure.

DOAN'S BACKACHE KIDNEY PILLS.

The **Kidney's duty** is to filter the blood and to take from all the waste matter and poisons—particularly the uric acid which it gathers in the course of its never-ceasing journey round the system.

Advert from the WOODBRIDGE REPORTER *in 1902*

As the sole end of matrimony is to propagate our species, it must be grievous to those who are coupled together and who, no doubt, wish for children, to be debarred of so great a blessing. Mrs. Gibson has a medicine which will remove every cause of barrenness and procure immediate conception. Ladies who have been married for twenty years and never had any children have become mothers by taking this noble medicine.

NORWICH MERCURY 1763

To young persons who have injured themselves by a destructive habit practised among boys in large schools are particularly recommended the Persian Restorative Drops prepared by J. Hodson M.D., 8s 6d a bottle. Sold by Chase & Co., Norwich and Marshall, Lynn.

NORFOLK CHRONICLE 1787

And just in case that last advert was not explicit enough, the GAZETTE had for sale in 1766 a book entitled *Onanism, a Treatise on the Disorders produced by Masturbation*, translated from the French and priced at two shillings.

It was hard to separate a genuine newspaper report from an advert as one could be designed to look like the other.

> *We hear from Carlisle that a gentleman of that county thinks it but justice to Dr. Ward of London to acquaint the publick that he has been lately cured of a dropsy by Dr. Ward's Powders after all other medicines had proved ineffectual and his case became desperate.*
>
> NORWICH MERCURY August 22nd 1752

It is also interesting to note just what was regarded as being healthy.

> **A FAIR TEETOTALLER** — *There is a married lady residing within 12 miles of Bath who has adopted the total abstinence principle for several years and has increased to the astonishing weight of 284 lbs. and yet is still active and energetic in the superintendence of her domestic duties.*
>
> LYNN ADVERTISER September 13th 1842

Living to a ripe old age was a good sign.

> *Last died at Chelsea, one John Roberts, aged 111; he was a soldier in King William's army at the Battle of the Boyne and served under the Duke of Marlborough in Queen Anne's wars.*
>
> NORWICH MERCURY January 11th 1772

Of course, if the last part of this was true, he was still a serving soldier at the age of nearly 50.

As time went on, medical advances attracted great interest. Jenner's vaccination was not universally acclaimed, especially by the church of the day. However, one letter to the NORFOLK CHRONICLE in February 1806 tried to put the case that *to inoculate is taking the work out of the hands of the Almighty'.*

Other attempts to drive health care forward could be overly optimistic.

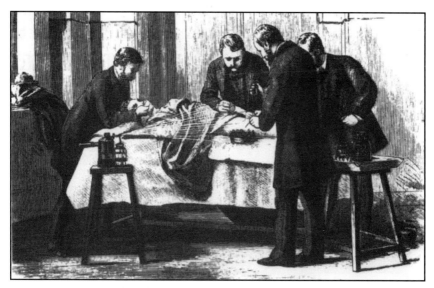

An operation using Lister's antiseptic spray to kill germs

From the University of Naples is reported the successful transfusion of blood by transferring arterial blood directly from the carotid artery of a living lamb put in communication with a vein in the arm of a woman suffering from a haemorrhage.

LYNN NEWS & COUNTY PRESS January 18th 1873

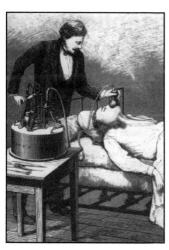

On Monday last, at the Lowestoft Infirmary, Dr. Worthington tested the value of Chloroform as a substitute for sulphuric aether in surgical operations, in the presence of several medical gentlemen of the neighbourhood. The following operations were performed under its influence.

Case 1: A poor woman of an extremely nervous and excitable temperament . . . submitted to the removal of a malignant tumour of the face.

Case 2: The middle finger with part of the hand was amputated in the case of a man, owing to a severe and protracted disease of the part . . .

Case 3: It is unnecessary to describe the particulars of this operation, sufficient to remark that had it not been for the anaesthetic influence of the Chloroform, it would otherwise have proved an exceedingly painful one.

NORWICH MERCURY December 11th 1847

Which just leaves us to contemplate what the last operation might have been.

A Victorian doctor's waiting room

Doctors, however, were not always held in the highest regard.

WHO WAS RIGHT? — *Two doctors came to examine the same patient. Both put both hands under the bedclothes to feel the pulse, but by accident got hold of each other's. 'This man has the Cholera,' said one. 'No such thing,' said the other, 'He's drunk.'*

SWAFFHAM JOURNAL March 1879

Following an operation carried out by Mr H. P. Helsham, surgeon of Beccles on a man named William Gray:

Mrs. Gray said . . . she and her daughter had to complain of the way it was carried out. The saw which Dr. Helsham used in severing the bone of her husband's leg was old and rusty and had been picked up on the heath where it had been thrown away as useless. Dr. Helsham never asked her consent nor that of her husband, and she had no idea that he intended to remove the foot. A portion of the diseased bone of the leg was now protruding from the flesh, and this would probably necessitate a second operation. Mrs. Baker, who held the patient's leg while the operation was being performed, produced the saw, which was handed over to the Board amid cries of 'shame!' She added that Dr. Helsham asked her if she could find a saw, saying that any old thing would do. He asked her to put some grease on it. With the exception of a pair of scissors, he had no surgical instruments whatever with him. She thought that the 'jar' from the saw must have caused Gray considerable pain, as he shrieked loudly several times during the operation. The foot was mortified and had been in that condition for some time. After the operation, Dr. Helsham threw the foot into the hearth and she subsequently took it into the churchyard and buried it . . . Dr. Helsham did not consider that the patient was in any fit state to be put under chloroform . . . He was unable to say whether the patient would recover or not.

NORFOLK WEEKLY STANDARD & ARGUS October 23rd 1897

However, key figures like Florence Nightingale and Elizabeth Garrett helped raise the profile, both of medicine as a career, and the place of women in that career.

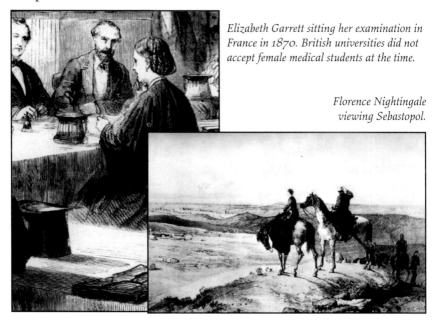

Elizabeth Garrett sitting her examination in France in 1870. British universities did not accept female medical students at the time.

Florence Nightingale viewing Sebastopol.

Cures could be effected or at least attempted by all kinds of people, including those with no real medical training.

BURY ST. EDMUNDS – A STRANGE DELUSION – *A remarkable case of mental hallucination has occurred in this town. A poor woman, the wife of a shepherd, fancied it had been revealed to her from heaven that she was neither to eat nor drink anything until she had another revelation commanding her to do so. Her husband and friends did all they could to remove the delusion, but all in vain, and on Thursday last, after she had remained six days without food, it was thought advisable to remove her to the Workhouse. Here, every attention was paid to her . . . and every delicacy which the Master (Mr. Rowland Dalton) could procure was kindly made use of to tempt her to eat . . . as her health was evidently failing and her pulse being imperceptible, some strong beef tea and port wine were administered by the stomach pump, for which considerable force was required. On Monday . . . being visited by the Rev. C. Elven, after praying with her, he enquired if she could repeat the Lord's Prayer, which she did, and he reminded her that if she was to ask for her daily bread, it was of course in order that she might eat it. No sooner was this suggestion made, than her countenance brightened up, and it seemed as if the scales had fallen from her eyes. She consented to eat . . . and she will probably have recovered from the effects in a few days.*
HALESWORTH TIMES February 3rd 1857

A QUACK IN TROUBLE – *Henry Clarke of Norwich, described as a tramp, was charged with acting as a pedlar without a licence at Cossey on the 23rd inst. The officer at Cossey the other day went into a public house in that village, and there found defendant sitting on a form alongside a farmer, who had lately been suffering from ill health. The defendant was engaged in a learned disquisition of the disease under which the other person was labouring, he pretending to know what it was. He dilated upon its disastrous effect to the system, its incurability by any medicine save the box of pills which he held in his hand, the therapeutic powers of which he never tired of extolling. Thirteen shillings was the small amount of money he asked for the box of pills. The wary farmer was not gulled, and the 'professor', no doubt anxious for the well-being of the bucolic system, offered*

*his box of pills first at 11s., and then at 1s 1¹/₂d! . . . For trading without
a pedlar's certificate . . . defendant was fined 5s and 13s costs; and a boy
who was in attendance was despatched to his 'Mrs.' for the money.*

DISS EXPRESS November 1st 1872

*A quack doctor visited our market on Wednesday last, and upon his rep-
resenting his pills, draughts and mixtures to be capable of curing all the
aches and complaints that the human flesh is heir to, a man in the crowd,
somewhat worse for drink . . . was induced to buy a box containing about
35 moderately sized pills. He emptied the entire contents of the box into
his mouth at once and swallowed the lot, without even making a wry face,
greatly to the amusement of the bystanders.*

THETFORD & WATTON TIMES & PEOPLE'S JOURNAL
October 14th 1882

Drugs have always had side-effects, as can be seen in this early case
of date-rape.

HORRIBLE ATROCITY – *Michael Shipman, a dissenter, a married
man and a man of property in Hinckley, Leics., was called to answer
the complaint of a beautiful girl named Emma Dalton . . . The indictment charged him with having assaulted Miss Dalton and administered
Laudanum or some other exciting drug for the purpose of producing
unconsciousness, insensibility or excitement in that young lady with the
view of rendering her subservient to his passions . . . The prosecutrix on
getting into the box, trembled exceedingly. In her countenance, which
wore the marks of thought and sorrow, could be traced the evidences of
former happiness. The spectators turned with horror to her abuser, who
presented a hideous contrast. His head was covered with lank red hair.
He, now and then grinned horribly a ghastly smile, especially when his
counsel was proceeding to draw inferences from the evidence, which led
him to entertain a vain hope.*

SUFFOLK CHRONICLE August 8th 1818

The judge, in his summing up, virtually instructed the jury to find
Shipman guilty. He was fined £100 and imprisoned for twelve months.

7
Dead and buried

When I began researching this book, it was astounding how many stories I gathered on this topic. There seemed to be a morbid fascination with the whole process of death. In the end I found it necessary to publish a separate book entitled *Grave Reports*. As a result only a few such items now appear in this book. But rest assured, it is almost impossible to open an eighteenth or nineteenth century newspaper without encountering a good story about coffins, graveyards or funerals.

For example, on the gravestone of an organist named Merideth, the BECCLES WEEKLY News of August 18th 1857 reported was engraved the following rhyme:

Here lies one blown out of breath
Who lived a merry life and died a Merideth

The NORFOLK NEWS in May 1845 announced the deaths on the same day of Mr and Mrs Pleasance who had lived at Redmoor Fen near Ely, at the ripe old ages of 107 and 105 respectively. They left a daughter of 84.

The practice of burying shipwrecked bodies in holes on the beach of the Norfolk coast without Christian burial is discontinued by the humane intervention of Mr. Munhall who was lately chosen one of the coroners of that county.
IPSWICH JOURNAL March 19th 1791

An inquest sat on the body of Charles Docking of Mildenhall, who was at play with some other children upon a gravestone in the churchyard there, when the stone broke, falling upon him, and killed him. Verdict – accidental death.

IPSWICH JOURNAL April 12th 1817

DEATH IN THE POT — *John Duncan, a pensioner, got drunk as usual on his pension and during the night got up in search of water. Coming over his bed, he fell head foremost into the kail-pot. He was found with his head in it next day quite dead.*

BURY & NORWICH POST April 25th 1832

Thursday died a man of the name of Etheringwood at a great age in Kent Street in the Borough, who maintained himself upwards of 40 years begging. On clearing his apartment of filth and old rags, property to the amount of £475 in gold, silver and halfpence was discovered sewed up in old cloaths, and in several crevices in the miserable apartments, and which was claimed by a relation in the neighbourhood as heir-at-law who never countenanced him in his lifetime; but to his disappointment, the thrifty mendicant had made a will in favour of a favourite woman who attended him in all his illness.

IPSWICH JOURNAL October 7th 1797

FALMOUTH — *Yesterday came in from Her Majesty's Ship, the Arundel, informing us that a ship from Virginia was lately driven on shore near Waterford, wherein there were found but 2 men alive, and the one of them had eaten the flesh of his arms through violent hunger.*

NORWICH GAZETTE December 21st 1706

A soldier of the garrison of Metz, dying lately there, the surgeons found in his bowels 1250 stones of cherries, plumbs and apricocks.

NORWICH MERCURY October 21st 1732

The way in which early local papers reported death and injury could be at some times lurid and graphic, on other occasions flippant and totally lacking in feeling.

NORWICH — *On Sunday morning, a young man, servant to Mrs. Ladell of Rackheath, going to shoot some crows in a field, the gun burst and shattered his hand to pieces; his thumb was found some time after, hanging on a tree by the sinew, which was several inches long.*

NORWICH MERCURY July 25th 1772

On Tuesday last, the following accident happened at Gissing near Diss; A child in the absence of its mother, approaching too near the fire, its clothes caught the flame, and before the mother's return, the child was burnt in so terrible a manner as to render assistance useless, and expired in a few hours in the greatest agonies, exhibiting a scene too shocking to hear or behold.

IPSWICH JOURNAL January 15th 1780

RINGSTEAD — *A few days ago, a sad accident occurred to Master Ed. Robertson, the son of Mr. Robertson, farmer, Ringstead. He being fond of a gun, went to scare birds, when charging some powder dropped on a piece of burning paper by his feet; by some mysterious means this caught the flask of powder which exploded, shattering the hand so much it is questionable if he ever recovers the use of it. Master Edward will get lots of sympathy, but unfortunately, his sympathisers cannot give him back his fingers.*

THE HUNSTANTON TELEPHONE August 3rd 1878

A farm bailiff named Jones, apparently for no better reason than to escape a possible action for breach of promise has committed suicide. He first tried a wash-tub, but finding this an unsavoury mode of making his exit, he escaped from the suds and hanged himself.

THETFORD & WATTON TIMES April 8th 1882

ELY ACCIDENT — *As a lad named Herbert Creak was chopping a piece of wood, to his astonishment, the first joint of the little finger of his left hand fell one way, and the piece of wood the other. His nervous system is not much shaken apparently, as he carries the dismembered joint about in his pocket to show to his most intimate companions.*

LYNN NEWS April 5th 1873

The NORWICH ARGUS for April 22nd 1865 described how two undertakers arrived to conduct a poor man's funeral in Dundee. The dead man, a flax-dresser named Peter Fyffee, was far too big for the coffin that had been brought, and the article describes in graphic detail the lengths the men went to to try to make the body fit, before finally admitting defeat and going in search of another coffin.

We have already seen how the HUNSTANTON TELEPHONE & WEST NORFOLK CHRONICLE could treat almost any subject as flippantly as possible. Take another example: the topic of cremation, addressed on March 10th 1882:

CREMATING HIM.

Dr. H. Crockerden, (who used to visit Huns'ton, and was well known, died in 1875,) requested Miss Williams to see his body cremated after death, and in his will authorized the payment of the expense. His relatives objected, and had him buried in Brompton Cemetery; but Miss Williams succeeded in getting it removed to Italy, and cremated him. She sued the Executors for the cost, but the Chancery Court has just decided against her. We suggest the lovely idea of cremation to our readers, and suggest that the Gas Co's. here and elsewhere should make use of their retorts for such purposes; it would add immensely to their profits.

'Tis sweet to love. but sweeter still,
Sometimes to lose your love ;
To find that he is cre--ma-ted,
And gone to Heaven above.
Before Cremation.

Doct-er Hen-e-ry Crockinden,
To fire, alas was fated ;
Not fire and brimstone do we mean—
But fire to be cremated.
After Cremation.

His ashes in the Urn in the Parlor, surrounded with pretty flowers is a charming idea. The said ashes could be handed round as snuff, on the annual cremating day, birthdays, &c. We give the hint gratuituously to Miss Williams and others.

At Cromer Museum it is possible to view copies of the CROMER TELEGRAPH, a hand-written daily newspaper, which appeared in September 1834. Though short-lived, it attempted to report an interesting mix of items, the best of which are local.

Express from Northrepps Hall: As a cannon was firing this (Tuesday) evening, in honour of Mr. E. Buxton's intended marriage with Miss

Upshaw of Sherringham, it, being too hard leaded, burst, and the unfortunate blacksmith who was firing it, was shot and fell down dead instantly, leaving a wife and five children to lament his loss.

CROMER TELEGRAPH September 4th 1834

Reports of bizarre deaths have always been worthy of column space.

A horrible accident by machinery has happened at Messrs Frys chocolate manufactory. While a young man was oiling the steam engine, one of the wheels caught his clothes and he was dragged into the midst of the machinery, his abdomen torn open and part of his intestines wound about the wheels.

NORFOLK NEWS July 10th 1847

From Killarney in the County of Kerry in Ireland, we are told that one Laughlin Brady lately attempted to rob an eagle's nest over the famous lake in that place, when the parent bird was in sight; the eagle flew at him with great fierceness upon which he tried to make a prudent retreat, but being too precipitate, he slipped from the rock and fell into the lake. This circumstance would not have been attended with any fatal consequence, as he was an excellent swimmer, had not the eagle pursued him into the water, and striking with unceasing fury at his head, reduced him to the necessity of diving every moment, so that he became quite exhausted at length, and was actually drowned. A neighbour of his, who was a witness of the whole transaction, but who, being neither a swimmer nor having a boat, was unable to assist him, gives this account of the affair; and 'tis remarkable, that when the body was taken out of the water, the eyes were picked out of the head and the whole face so dreadfully mangled, that a more shocking spectacle could not be raised up to imagination.

IPSWICH JOURNAL April 4th 1767

A few days since, a little boy about 4 years old, son of a person named Cone, living at Melton, was discovered feet upwards in a muck bin, where he had by some means accidentally fallen in. He had not been missing long, but when found was quite dead, suffocation having no doubt speedily terminated the misery of his horrible situation.

SUFFOLK CHRONICLE May 21st 1842

NEWCASTLE — *On Saturday night last, a servant of Mr Barker's of Sebraham, in serving up his master's horse, got hold of a man's foot amongst the hay. He ran away affrighted, to inform his master, who imagining there were thieves, took a gun and went to the place and asked who was there, and was answered, 'I'll soon let you know,' which Mr. Barker, taking as a threat, shot the man in his groin. The unfortunate young man happens to be a neighbour to Mr. Barker, who had made an appointment to meet a girl in that place. He got home, and died on Monday, but freely forgave Mr. Barker who is himself almost distracted for what has happened.*

IPSWICH JOURNAL March 29th 1777

Thursday, a very promising young woman, but lately from the country, died suddenly at the house of her uncle in Spa fields, in consequence of a fright which she received from a cousin, who, out of wantonness, contrived to come down the chimney of the chamber in which she slept.

IPSWICH JOURNAL May 3rd 1800

On Tuesday afternoon, a shocking accident occurred from the top of the Nelson Monument on the South Denes [Yarmouth]. *A professional singer and acrobat named Charles Marsh, accompanied by another professional named Wharton, went up to the Monument to have a view from the top. From the platform, Marsh got outside and clambered up to the figure of Britannia which stands 14 feet on the summit. At this giddy height, he began to perform some of his gam-*

The Yarmouth Nelson monument

bols (one man playing on the banjo, the other on the violin), in the course of which he missed his hold and fell headlong from the trident to the ground, a distance of 140 feet, and was of course dashed to pieces at the foot of the pillar.

YARMOUTH INDEPENDENT May 20th 1863

At the inquest following this last tragedy, Wharton denied they had been inebriated *'or we would not have been able to play while walking up the steps'.* The verdict was that Marsh had been accidentally killed.

If that was unfortunate, what came about in the same town 18 years earlier was far worse. In May 1845, a circus clown by the name of Nelson announced that he would sail up the river in a tub drawn by four geese. Hundreds turned out to watch, lining both sides of the river. Arguably, those with the best view were crowded onto the suspension bridge on the North Quay which spanned the River Bure. Some even climbed up on the chains and suspenders of the bridge. *'The chains snapped and the bridge and occupants plummeted into the water . . . so quick was it that not a scream was heard'* (NORFOLK NEWS May 10th 1845). Though boats were launched immediately, at least 80 died, mostly women and children.

Even after death, people could cause problems.

CURIOUS MISTAKE — *A few days since, an inmate of the Eye Union House died and the Governor sent word to the authorities of the parish of Occold that he would be buried there on a certain day, and to have them prepare a grave for him. Accordingly, the old sexton, who varies the monotony of bell-ringing with digging graves, immediately set to work. After a time it was discovered that Occold was not the proper place to bury the departed in, but Redlingfield was the parish to which he belonged. Therefore messengers were at once despatched — the one to Occold to say that the grave would not be required, and the other to Redlingfield to have a grave prepared. The poor man at Occold talks of sueing for costs. He says the grave thrown upon his hands is no earthly use to him and he thinks he ought to be paid for his trouble.*

Yarmouth Gazette February 13th 1875

WRECK OF NYMPHA PRIZE ON SUSSEX COAST — [Under this heading, the Norwich Mercury described the arrival of thousands to the shore to plunder the vessel, but the weather being so cold, some died there of exposure. As an aside we are told —] *A woman at Seaford whose husband being dead at the wreck, hired a cart and horse to fetch him in order to bury him, but the carter not knowing him brought her another man instead of her husband, upon which the woman refused to pay the carter and he left her the man.*

Norwich Mercury December 12th 1747

8

The weather

It is not a new phenomenon for the English to be fascinated by the weather. It was always newsworthy, especially when it was particularly extreme.

NAYLAND TEMPEST — *On Friday morning, a tempest of unusual severity passed directly over this village, during which time the rain fell in torrents. The lightning was very vivid and almost incessant, with very heavy peals of thunder. A small fir tree, near the coal yard, was struck by the electric fluid, but a man and boy who were at work close by, escaped unhurt.*

STOWMARKET COURIER September 16th 1869

BUNGAY — *This town and neighbourhood was visited with rather a severe tempest on Saturday afternoon, the 3rd inst. The lightning was very vivid and we learn that a poor woman at Denton, whilst cutting some bread for her children's tea, was struck — the electric fluid being attracted by the blade of the knife.*

BECCLES WEEKLY NEWS April 13th 1858

On Tuesday last, at Woodbridge, there was a more violent hailstorm accompanied by thunder and rain than had ever been remembered at so late a period of the year by the oldest person living. The houses in several parts of the town were flooded, and such was the quantity of hail that the

boys pelted each other with it all the afternoon as though it had been in the depth of winter.

SUFFOLK CHRONICLE August 3rd 1816

We have the following remarkable account by private letters from Moscow that by the excessive cold, one hundred persons were froze to death in the streets, great numbers of birds fell down dead with their wings expanded, and two horses left before a brandy shop were frozen to death harnessed to their sledges, but not discerned to be dead till their masters came to drive them and [they] appeared as living, but stiff as wood.

IPSWICH GAZETTE March 10th 1733

Yesterday se'nnight between the hours of twelve and one, a violent storm, attended with lightning, hail and rain, came on at Trimley, which lasted about an hour. Mr. Pooley's son, Robert, a miller of that place, in endeavouring to shut one of the mill windows, was struck with a flash of light-

ning. He remained senseless for some time, and is so terribly burnt that his life is thought to be in great danger. It is remarkable that altho' he was withinside the mill, his toes were blistered and his stockings singed.

IPSWICH JOURNAL April 24th 1783

During a recent thunderstorm, a shower of frogs fell from one of the sur-charged clouds over the Humber. Several dropped onto the decks of vessels navigating the river and a portion of the coast . . . was for a time covered by myriads of strange arrivals.

NORFOLK NEWS July 11th 1846

The postman who went from Bury to Thetford lost himself in the snow, and when he had got some distance from the road, his horse sunk into a bog up to his belly; in this state he remained till the morning. The Stoke post was obliged to return and the Brandon lad and his horse were dug out of the snow.

IPSWICH JOURNAL February 21st 1784

WYMONDHAM — *On Wednesday last between the hours of 5 and 6 o'clock in the afternoon, we had a most violent tempest of thunder and lightning. The lightning struck the East end of Becket's Chapel, now the Free Grammar School, and beat down the weather-cock with a large ball of stone on which it stood, broke the window, split the freestone quoins and very much shattered the whole end of the building. Part of the same flash entered a dwelling house in the same street in which were several persons, one of whom, a woman, was struck down and very much burnt, but is now in a fair way of recovery.*

NORWICH MERCURY August 17th 1777

Capel school destroyed by lightning

IPSWICH — *The electrical disturbance of the atmosphere on Thursday last, which was so severely felt in different parts of this county was attended with a terrible catastrophe at Capel [St Mary] near this town, the National School being struck whilst the children were assembled therein, the master [Mr Alexander] and boys all receiving the concussion and 3 of the children losing their lives, whilst several others were seriously injured and the building itself was destroyed.*

BURY & NORWICH POST August 16th 1854

The account told of how the boys' room had received a direct hit, whilst the girl pupils had escaped more lightly. The three dead were named as William Scrivener (7) of Capel, John Kettle (9) of Belstead and Walter Cook (10) of Capel.

On Thursday morning, the 8th inst., the inhabitants of the village of Blythburgh were much frightened by a long rumbling noise followed by a great shock. On looking for the cause of this noise, they discovered that the ruins of the walls of the old priory of St. Augustine had been levelled to the ground. It had long resisted the rough tempestuous winds by which it had been so frequently assailed, and at last on a calm summer day, it fell beneath the hoary weight of old age, leaving one less of the mementoes of the good old times that have gone by.

BECCLES & BUNGAY WEEKLY NEWS June 20th 1865

Dreadful storms hit the East coast from time to time leading to great loss of life. The DOWNHAM MARKET GAZETTE reported on November 6th 1880 the loss of the Wells lifeboat, which had capsized with the loss of eleven lives. That same night a week earlier, the Sheringham fishing lugger the *Gleaner,* ended up bottom upwards on the beach by Beeston Church with the loss of ten fishermen.

The fishing towns of Suffolk and Norfolk expected tragedy to strike on a regular basis. The old folk song 'Three Score and Ten' tells of the freak storm of February 1889, when huge numbers of lives were lost. This song was written and copies were sold to raise money for the bereaved families.

Remembering the loss of the Wells lifeboat 125 years on, in October 2005

Methinks I see a host of craft,
Spreading their sails at lee
As down the Humber they do steer,
Down for the great North Sea
Me thinks I see a wee small craft
And crew with hearts so brave
They go to earn their daily bread
Upon the restless waves.

And it's three score and ten
Boys and men were lost from Grimsby Town
From Yarmouth down to Scarborough
Many hundreds more were drowned
Their herring craft and trawlers
Their fishing smacks as well
Alone they fight the bitter night
And battle with the swell.

The LOWESTOFT JOURNAL on February 16th 1889 told of ships lost all along the East coast. The report spoke of deck hands washed overboard, crews rescued from sinking vessels, severe damage and loss of life. This story was then a week old, but more was to unfold. On February 23rd, the same paper described how a pair of fishing smacks out of Yarmouth were back at sea when the *Angela* landed a body in her trawl net. It was the son of the skipper of the other boat, a boy named Lawson. Much was made of the bad luck that was supposed to befall a ship landing a body in this way. A happier tale was that of a Lowestoft smack, the *Tantivy*, assumed lost with all hands. The LOWESTOFT JOURNAL was able to report that the gale had carried the small boat across the North Sea to Holland where a miraculous rescue had been accomplished, described in flowing prose:

She was blown onto her beam-ends and the ballast, which consisted of shingle, was shifted . . . The wind blew colder and louder and a fearful sea was running. So high were the waves that a vessel that came quite close to them could not be seen when she was down in the hollow. The men were almost blinded with the snow squalls. The hailstones that fell were about as big as marbles and cut like knives. They were helpless in the grip of the storm, and were driven towards the Dutch coast. The wind was as pitiless as the hand of death and the men were almost frozen with the cold. The mate [John Edmunds] was caught by the roaring gale and flung into the little boat. He was deluged with water. Another man [Edward Matthews] was thrown among the ballast and buried up to his neck in the shingle. It was some time before the men succeeded in digging him out . . . They turned their attention to the safety of the ship. From the weather side, the crew could almost see the keel of the vessel. The foam-crested billows swept the deck and the poor fellows had the greatest difficulty in holding on, so furious was the gale and so violent the seas that swept over them.

The rescue itself was no less dramatic. A Dutch ship manoeuvred alongside and as the *Tantivy* rose up with the waves, most of the men were able to jump onto their rescuer's boat. Even the ship's cat was saved. Last to be saved were the Master, William Shilling,

A wreck at Gorleston

and the boy who were hauled from the water, one by his hair, the other by his guernsey. They were cared for in a first-class hotel.

Throughout January 1895 the LOWESTOFT WEEKLY PRESS reported on storms and gales, and lives lost. Lifeboat rescues, the sinking of fishing boats, flooding along the coast, shipwrecks off Southwold and Cromer, as well as disasters in the Humber, all filled the columns that month. Worse was to follow. On January 30th 1895, two steamships, the *Elbe* and the *Crathie,* were in collision in fog, 45 miles off Lowestoft. According to first reports, the *Elbe* lost 374 of its 395 passengers and crew. The 21 survivors clung to wreckage long enough to be picked up by the fishing smack, *Wildflower.* The LOWESTOFT WEEKLY PRESS reported for weeks about bodies and debris being washed ashore. On May 4th, the inquest found the accident had been caused largely as a result of gross negligence on the part of the mate and look-out on the *Crathie.* However, Lloyd, the German own-

ers of the *Elbe,* had advised surviving officers not to attend the inquest or the Board of Trade inquiry, so it was hard to assess the *Elbe*'s part in the accident. Praise was reserved for the Captain, William Wright, and crew of the smack *Wildflower* for rescuing the survivors in perilous conditions. A reward fund was instituted for these heroes. Gold medals were sent to the Captain and crew of the *Wildflower* from New York (LOWESTOFT WEEKLY PRESS June 8th 1895).

Tragedy could occur within yards of the shore:

CLEY ‑ *On Thursday the 16th inst. the Russell of Yarmouth, Nicholas Fray, Master, from London, in ballast was lost on the King's Sand, near the harbour's mouth. The ship was broke to pieces and the crew, which consisted of 7 persons, all perished.*

NORWICH MERCURY January 21st 1772

The storm yesterday fortnight at Lowestoft was most melancholy. A brig foundered near the shore and laid in such a position that no efforts could relieve the crew (eight in number): they clung to the wreck, and their cries during the evening were distinctly heard in the streets. They all perished within a few yards, as it were, of almost the whole population of Lowestoft.

SUFFOLK CHRONICLE January 1st 1820

A MESSAGE FROM THE SEA — *A bottle was picked up on our coast a few days ago, containing the following note – 'February 14th Barque Queen of South Shields, waterlogged off Cromer, and expecting to founder any minute, blowing a heavy gale at East, God spare us. Whoever picks*

this up, make it known at Shields.' — The vessel is believed to have been lost with all hands in the late terrible gales.

STOWMARKET COURIER
March 3rd 1870

But even by North Sea standards, 1789 must have been the worst of all years. Norfolk papers were full of the unprecedented storms of November that year, when 120 bodies were washed ashore between Yarmouth and Cromer, the result of 40 fishing boats lost.

9

New inventions

As early as 1790, the NORFOLK CHRONICLE was advertising for sale *'the new Patent Portable Washing Machine'*, guaranteed to be *'universally useful and economical'.* It was said it could wash more than ten women could in the same time.

The ability of machines to make workers redundant was an issue that would give rise to riot and unrest, especially as nineteenth century inventiveness asserted itself.

DISTURBANCE AT GOSBECK — *It is with the deepest regret we learn that a riotous disposition has shewn itself in the parish of Gosbeck near this town (Ipswich). We trust . . . that this spirit so subversive of good order, so contrary to the laws of the country and so ruinous and danger-ous to themselves is confined to a very limited number. On Tuesday last, however, about twenty deluded persons assembled, and in a wanton and most disorderly manner, destroyed two threshing machines in the above parish, and threatened to destroy others.*

SUFFOLK CHRONICLE February 25th 1815

When the rioters were brought to trial they were each tried and found guilty on one count of destroying a threshing machine and imprisoned for one month. The other count was left pend-ing. They were strongly warned that any repeat of such behaviour would lead to a far stronger sentence. However, new technology was fast developing in all walks of life.

An exhibition was made at Lowestoft of the new-invented lamp to give light to ships out at sea; it consists of 1,000 small mirrors, fed by oil, which reflect the light. It answered beyond expectation, and is much superior to the present light-houses. A ship was sent out to sea, when the people on board saw it many minutes before they could the lighthouse. At four leagues distance, it appeared like a globe of fire in the air.

IPSWICH JOURNAL July 11th 1778

On Tuesday, an experiment was made in Harwich Harbour of the patent life-preserving mattress by a man named Goodwin belonging to the alien-office boat, who plunged into the sea from one of the breakwaters: about one third of his person was above the surface of the water and no exertion of either hands or feet was required — it forms a complete mattress for a bed whilst it possesses also the life saving property . . . affixing it to the body will occupy about a minute.

SUFFOLK CHRONICLE March 6th 1813

The SUFFOLK CHRONICLE in June 1849, just prior to the Great Exhibition, was advertising 'Idrotobolic Hats,' guaranteed to prevent pain and headaches on account of their special ventilation system.

Also you could buy *'The Newly Invented Spectacles with a built in Organic Vibrator to counteract deafness.'*

> *The comfort of travellers by the Great Northern Railway has been greatly increased this winter by the introduction of iron foot-warmers filled with hot water into all first-class carriages.*
>
> NORFOLK NEWS January 24th 1852

The STOWMARKET COURIER reported in February 1870 that the Stowmarket Gun Cotton Company had supplied a large quantity of explosive to blast rock in the building of the Suez Canal. As we know, that came into being, conceived and engineered by Ferdinand de Lesseps. Not all good ideas were so workable.

> *The desert of Sahara has been visited by Mr. de Lesseps who has been investigating the possibilities of creating an inland sea in the desert by admitting the waters of the Mediterranean.*
>
> SWAFFHAM JOURNAL January 4th 1877

Not all inventions were great successes. Take for example one article from the THETFORD WEEKLY POST of December 22nd 1905 where it was suggested it would soon be possible to row through the skies in a cigar-shaped gas bag propelled by a pair of wing-like oars driven by the aeronaut. *'The gravity is overcome by the use of the oars. It is stated that a speed from 4–6 miles per hour can be attained.'*

By the latter part of the nineteenth century, many local papers carried a science column. There was a real belief that science and invention would solve all the world's problems. The NORFOLK WEEKLY STANDARD & ARGUS for April 3rd 1897 in its science column described the use of Roentgen rays *'for discovering the position of foreign substances in the body,'* the invention of a frost-proof water pipe, the discovery that a microbe was responsible for baldness and the assertion that life on Mars was a distinct possibility.

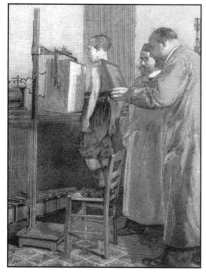

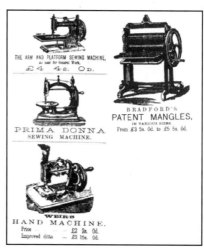

Roentgen examining a photographic plate

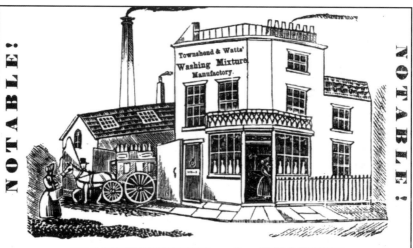

TOWNSHEND & WATTS'
UNEQUALLED
WASHING AND BLEACHING MIXTURE,
For Washing Linen, Flannels, Prints, &c.

This celebrated Composition is offered to the Public as the best Article ever invented for Washing and thoroughly Cleansing every description of Linen, Woollen, and Cotton Textures; its superlative Properties being beautifully exhibited in the dazzling Whiteness (the result of its searching and bleaching qualities) imparted to every description of Garment, and it should be carefully borne in mind, that by its peculiar action, the Hardest Spring Water is rendered equally available for service with Pipe or Rain Water.

9
Transport

Much in the world of invention and technology involved trans-port enabling people to move faster, further or merely to be more intrepid. The IPSWICH JOURNAL for September 13th 1783 recorded the Montgolfiers' first public flight of their balloon, which was said to have drawn *'all Paris together at the Champ de Mars'.* It flew a distance of four leagues before dropping and landing safely. As the reporter added, *'To what account this discovery may turn, cannot be ascertained, but much is expected from it here.'*

> *Yesterday Se'nnight between 7 and 8 in the evening, a fire balloon got entangled with the branches of a tree belonging to Mrs Hamby in St. Mary Elms in this town which set it on fire, but soon went out, tho' not before the neighbourhood were very much alarmed, the tree being near a haystack; in consequence of which the magistrates the next day prohibited the use of fire balloons in this town in future.*
> IPSWICH JOURNAL October 2nd 1784

Two air balloons had been launched from the bowling green in Ipswich the previous week, *'affording entertainment to a vast concourse of people'.* Mr Decker, at Norwich sent up a manned air balloon the following May (Parson James Woodforde mentions this in his famous diary). From the descriptions in the Norfolk papers, the beauty and magnificence of the gondola it carried was a sight worth seeing, *'it being richly embellished and decorated in a style of unparalleled elegance'*, so much so that it struggled to carry *'Mr. Decker and a young lady from London'.* Large sums were paid for tickets to view the event. A year later, people had come to realise you did not have to pay handsomely to see a balloon fly above your head.

NORWICH – *Saturday being the day fixed for the ascension of Major Money, Mr. Lockwood and Captain Blake in an air balloon from Quantrell's Gardens, . . . the county and city members and numbers of other gentlemen and ladies assembled upon the occasion and a vast concourse of people in the streets and on the tops of houses. Despite bad weather, and the balloon refusing to ascend, as well as getting entangled in a tree, it was decided to remove most of the ballast and allow Major Money to make the journey on his own. After this, the balloon got into a different current*

of air, which carried it directly over the city . . . As he passed over his own house, Crown Point, Trowse Newton, the guns in the park were fired, but the Major was too high to hear them . . . A little before six, the balloon was seen at a prodigious height at Lowestoft, making towards the continent. It was the Major's intention to have gone but a few miles. When he found himself going towards the sea, he opened the valve to let himself down but the air escaped too slowly.

Climbing up the ropes the intrepid Major used his knife to open up the balloon, at which point it rapidly dropped landing him in the sea. There he remained for five and a half hours gradually sinking.

With a presence of mind superior to most men in such a perilous situation, he cut a hole in the sleeve of his coat into which he put his watch that he might know the time. Whilst in this dreadful suspense, a Dutch ship passed him but would render him no relief. At last, a boat belonging to the Argus Cutter, Captain Haggis, hailed him. The Major told the men he was a gentleman in distress in a balloon; they went back to their ship to make known the circumstance to the Captain, who immediately lent every assistance in his power. When taken up, the Major was eighteen miles distance from Southwold.

IPSWICH JOURNAL July 30th 1785

The balloon was recovered and brought back to Major Money's home at Trowse, where about seven hundred people paid 2s 6d for the benefit of seeing it whilst it was drying in the park. The money was collected for the benefit of the Norfolk and Norwich Hospitals.

Not all balloon journeys ended so favourably. The IPSWICH JOURNAL for July 29th 1837 described the death of Mr Cocking, as he attempted a descent from a balloon using a parachute of his own design. The balloon was launched from Vauxhall Gardens in London and rose to 5,000 feet before Mr Cocking, riding in a basket beneath the parachute, cut himself loose. The article described how he plummeted and was literally dashed to pieces, breathing his last just as his friends found his body. Heartless souvenir hunters attempted to carry off pieces of the basket as he lay dying.

Travel was the adventure of the age. The SWAFFHAM JOURNAL in January 1879 told of one Mr De Hars, American Consul in Alexandria, who had travelled around the world in just 63 days. This was six years after Jules Verne had suggested in his book that it might be done in 80.

For most of the period covered by this book, travelling by coach was the most likely way of getting about, though even that could prove a bit of an adventure, as this story from the SUFFOLK CHRONICLE of June 1824 shows.

RIVAL WHIPS.— Yesterday week, when the Phenomena and Times Coaches arrived at Scole Inn, on their way from Norwich to London, an altercation took place between the coachmen. in consequence of one of them charging the other with passing him on the road in an uncoachman-like manner, which could be settled in no other way than by the *fashionable* mode adopted by Spring and Langan, and the combatants leaving their coaches and passengers, stripped and set-to.—The combat lasted but a short time, for after 3 or 4 rounds, one of the gentlemen having received a *thorough-good* dressing. mounted his box, and made the best of his way to London. whilst the victor's passengers were heard to sing the well-known air—" *Here's to ye, Mr. Wiggins.*" A proprietor being on one of the coaches, seconded his coachee, but we have heard some complaints of an *unfair start.—* (*Bury Post.*)

Road accidents were plentiful and often fatal. At inquests that followed, the word 'inebriated' often featured. Not so in this case though:

On Saturday noon, as Mr. Chapman's servant of Attleborough was driving home his master's team laden with coals, and about a mile from Norwich, his foot slipped and, unable to recover himself, he fell down at full length, and both wheels of the wagon passing entirely along his back, he was so dreadfully crushed as to survive but a very few minutes. He was a young man and has left a wife and a family to lament his untimely death, but they have the consolation of knowing that the deceased was perfectly sober at the time of the accident.

IPSWICH JOURNAL
November 18th 1809

I am sure it was a great comfort to them.

The SUFFOLK CHRONICLE for September 14th 1822 reported that three days earlier, a massive robbery had taken place from the Ipswich mail coach. Gradually the story unravelled. A valuable parcel appeared to have been stolen or lost. It contained bank notes amounting to over £31,000 printed for Alexander's Banks at Ipswich, Needham Market, Woodbridge, Hadleigh and Manningtree. Immediately a reward was offered of £1,000. On October 5th 1822 the IPSWICH JOURNAL carried an advert announcing a reward of £5,000, stating that the missing notes would be rendered useless as they had been printed in black, and reprinted notes had now been delivered printed in red. The IPSWICH JOURNAL of October 19th 1822 announced a reduction in the reward to £2,000 following the recovery of most of the notes. Though the adverts continued until mid December, the thieves were never caught.

There were regular reports of communications hit by the

weather. Floods and deep snow could make already-bad roads impassable. But the mail was still expected to get through.

The weather in the last week of 1836 must have been some of the worst ever seen in East Anglia. Here is one small selection of details reported in the SUFFOLK CHRONICLE that show how things were for those unfortunate enough to be travelling at the time.

EFFECTS OF THE SNOW STORM IN SUFFOLK — *We are informed by our messenger who left Bury St. Edmunds at 9 o'clock yesterday morning, that the snow on that road has drifted to such an extreme height that the summit of some of the heaps could not be reached by the point of a stick three feet in length, extended at the extreme length of his arm although he raised himself as high as possible in the stirrups of the saddle for the purpose of trying the experiment. Various gangs of labourers were employed on different parts of the line in clearing away the snow. At Haughley not less than 118 men were at work for the purpose as he passed through that place.*

The Halesworth road beyond Saxmundham is even now nearly impassable and we understand that the Shannon coach on Tuesday became so deeply embedded in the snow, at a place called Brakes Lane, between Yoxford and Halesworth, as to render its extrication impossible, was abandoned like a foundered ship until the weather should have sufficiently moderated so as to lessen the difficulty of digging it out from its situation.

To give an idea of the bad condition between Ipswich and Needham Market it need only be stated that a van drawn by four horses, which was one more than usual, was seven hours in travelling a distance of 7 miles only.

On Thursday, the posts for Norwich were dispatched under the care of Jas. Cooper by post-chaise. It was soon found however that the roads were impassable by any vehicle beyond Stonham. He was therefore under the necessity of procuring a horse, and he proceeded onward with his load, which filled 2 sacks, towards his destination.

SUFFOLK CHRONICLE December 31st 1836

The Magpie inn at Stonham, around the end of the nineteenth century

As railways and other forms of road transport developed, so too did the deaths and injuries resulting from accidents.

CLARE – A NOCTURNAL ADVENTURE – *Early on Thursday morning last when Superintendent Bardwell was just reaching home from the fire at Hundon Hall, his mare suddenly swerved to one side, and, on getting down to ascertain the cause, our superintendent found a tricycle* *standing in the road, unlighted and unattended; further search discovered the owner wandering about near the post office corner, whither he had been attracted by the solitary lamp which is left burning all night. It transpired that the rider's lamp had gone out, and that, getting down in the dark, he had lost his steed and couldn't tell where to find it, and, for some two or three hours, had been engaged in the fruitless search. Mr. Bardwell conducted the stranger to his machine, and saw him fairly started with lamp alight, and, as nothing more was heard, we may presume that he completed his journey without further mishap.*

STOWMARKET COURIER January 30th 1890

COGGESHALL — *On Monday evening, Mr. William Saunders, milkman and seed grower, was walking from Kelvedon when he became so* *confused by the bright lights of Messrs. Moore's omnibus . . . that he failed to get out of the way, and was knocked down by the omnibus, the wheels passing over his arms and legs . . . Under the skilful treatment of Doctors Simpson*  *and Applebee, he is progressing satisfactorily.*

STOWMARKET COURIER January 2nd 1890

The DISS EXPRESS for September 25th 1874 informed its readers of the scandal of death and injury on our railways, with a thousand or more dying on the railways each year and 25,000 injured annually. Following a collision at Thorpe near Norwich, where a man named George Womack died, two railway officials were tried for manslaughter. Alfred Cooper, the Night Inspector, was found guilty and given 8 months' hard labour. John Robson, the telegraph clerk, was acquitted. According to the YARMOUTH GAZETTE reporting on the trial in April 1875, over £40,000 had been paid out by the railway company to those survivors injured in the crash. The

Thorpe station, Norwich

death toll continued, with the THETFORD & WATTON TIMES in 1882 listing weekly the deaths and injuries resulting from such accidents.

The tunnel by Ipswich station

The boiler of a train that exploded at Westerfield near Ipswich in 1900, killing both the driver, John Barnard, and the fireman, William MacDonald.

Disaster at sea was nothing new, but the loss of the steamship *Atlantic* in 1873 demonstrated just how many lives could be lost at once. The LYNN NEWS in April of that year described how 560 lives were lost off Halifax, including a number of local people. Again the statistics were grim reading. In the previous 32 years, 44 steamships had been lost in Atlantic crossings from Europe. Particularly perilous was the coast of Nova Scotia.

11

Animals, wild and tame

We are well known as a nation of animal lovers, so it comes as no surprise to discover that here was another topic that yielded up a vast collection of good stories.

On Friday last, as a woman was hoeing potatoes in a field at Horningsheath near this town (Bury), a swarm of bees alighted upon her head and were hived from thence, without her being in the least stung or injured.

BURY POST June 26th 1799

The Thoroughfare at Woodbridge, seen in a photograph taken at about the period of the news story below

AN UNWELCOME VISITOR – *On Saturday afternoon, as some bullocks were being driven through the Thoroughfare, one of them coolly walked into Mr. A. Scarfe's drapery establishment, to the amazement of those who were inside. It had a good look round and quietly turned round and walked out without doing the slightest damage. It then crossed the road and went into Mr. Peachey's shop, but evidently not finding the object of its search, came out, luckily doing no harm to anything or anybody.*

WOODBRIDGE REPORTER June 28th 1887

Mr. Robt. Woolterton of Loddon in Norfolk had a puppy lately given to him by a friend, supposing it to be old enough to lap; but after repeated trials without effect, it wandered about the yard and at last got to a sow and pigs; and it has ever since been nourished by the sow as one of her own.

SUFFOLK CHRONICLE January 6th 1816

A TOAD IN A BOY'S STOMACH — *About three o'clock on Friday morning, a boy, nine years of age, named Jonathan Micklethwaite . . . parted with a toad. The reptile, which was alive, was put into a basin of water and has since become much swollen. Its body now measures about three and a half inches long, two broad, and in colour is dark brown streaked with black. The boy for some weeks past has been worn almost to a skeleton, and perfectly ravenous in regard to food, constantly eating and never seeming satisfied. The medical attendant on the family says the boy must have swallowed the toad in spawn.*

BURY FREE PRESS August 15th 1857

The NORWICH MERCURY carried regular animal stories including one on August 3rd 1754 about a swordfish that had rammed a ship,

running his horn through timbers ten inches thick, and also this amazing attraction:

THE LEARNED FRENCH DOG *from Paris, that has been shewn at London all the Winter with such general applause is now to be seen at the Angel in the Market Place. This extraordinary dog has been seen with the greatest wonder and surprise by Kings, Princes and several Potentates abroad, as well as by several of the Royal Family, Nobility & Gentry of London, all allowing that the performance surpasses thought. Note: he reads, writes & casts accounts by the means of typographical cards.*

NORWICH MERCURY October 19th 1751

A RAT STORY – *a remarkable rat story comes from a couple who had been bothered by rats and mice playing tag in the dining room, and set a trap to catch them. Late that night, the husband, hearing queer noises, stole down to the room. What he saw, he describes in these words: about a dozen small mice had been caught in the trap. This was surrounded by four or five big rats, which had dragged it to one corner, and were hold-ing a consultation. As I looked in, alarmed by the light, they hurried their preparations to a close. One of the big fellows seized the door of the trap between his teeth; another rat seized him by the tail, another and another quickly took hold; a sudden pull was given, and quicker than I can relate, the door flew back, the mice scampered out, and before I could walk across the room, old rats, young rats, old mice, young mice, had disappeared, leaving the trap in the corner with the door shut, and every vestige of the bait gone.*

STOWMARKET COURIER January 9th 1890

*A rat pit where dogs were set upon large numbers of rats
that had been caught alive for the purpose*

In another rat story, the LYNN ADVERTISER of August 16th 1842 told of a rat-catcher in Bath who had collected the tails of all the rats he had killed (presumably as proof of his success) and was exhibiting them, all 43 bushels of them, including 30 perfectly white rats. The same paper, a fortnight later, described the capture of a whale which had come close to the harbour at King's Lynn. Apparently, *'one of the fishermen, Mr. William Chase, has had experience in the Greenland Fishery'.* The article spoke of *'hundreds wending their way thither to Ferry Boat Landing to view this formidable monster of the deep'.* They were being charged 2*d* a time.

This picture shows another whale, this time landed on Winterton beach in 1857.

CANINE SAGACITY — *Mr. John Freeman of Framsden, sometime since, gave to Mr. Charles Freeman, of Stowupland a mastiff bitch which is now kept by him and which regularly goes twice a week from Stowupland to the parish of Framsden (in the night), thereby establishing a post between the two parties, being a distance of about nine miles. Letters are secured upon the dog's neck in the evening by Mr. Freeman of Stowupland, and are received by Mr. Freeman of Framsden the following morning. The dog remains during the day, never longer, and returns to Stowupland, where letters are received the succeeding morning.*

Suffolk Chronicle August 31st 1822

A cod landed on the East Coast when opened was found to contain a ring, two keys, a pocket-knife with a bone handle, and 131 fish-hooks with line attached.

SWAFFHAM JOURNAL
January 18th 1879

A gentleman residing near the road has for the convenience of the postman had his letters . . . *deposited in a hole cut out of a post. The gentleman's servant went as usual to fetch the letters, and found the whole* [lot] *laid in a ditch near the spot. Upon examination, the servant found a woodpecker had made her nest in the post and had drawn out the letters and dropped them into the ditch. Fortunately no loss has been sustained through this mischievous bird.*

IPSWICH JOURNAL August 3rd 1816

LOWESTOFT – *On Saturday morning, a little boy, whilst passing down Rant's Score, was seized by a huge rat. The poor boy was much frightened by this unlooked-for encounter, but Mr. Matcham, driving down the score at the moment, jumped out of his gig and killed the animal.*

BECCLES & BUNGAY WEEKLY NEWS June 20th 1865

Mr. Nicholls farmer at Kelvedon found his pigeons in a very disturbed state and his dove-cot almost deserted as a pair of owls had taken up residence. The owls, it is almost needless to say, were very plump.

IPSWICH AND COLCHESTER TIMES April 29th 1859

This interest in animals was particularly noticeable where wildlife was concerned. Unfortunately, it usually meant the death of the creature concerned. Rare sightings of birds and animals regularly made the local newspapers. The IPSWICH JOURNAL reported the shooting of a hoopoe in Ipswich in 1797. Two dolphins were shot by Mr. J. Cobbold in the Orwell, and exhibited at the Coach and Horses in September 1816.

RARE BIRD — *A female specimen of the Bittern was killed last Saturday at Ramsholt by a man in the employ of Mr. Wm. Last. As is usual with this bird, it remained still enough for the man to approach and disable it with a stone. It may be seen . . . at Mr. Heffer's St. John's Street. Woodbridge, whither it has been sent for preservation.*

IPSWICH & COLCHESTER TIMES
February 11th 1859

At Holt, a golden Eagle was shot and given to a local taxidermist, Mr. C. Dack, who has had recently 47 Pomeraine Skua Gulls, 2 Richardson's Skuas, 2 Buffon's Skuas, 2 Peregrine Falcons, 2 Fulmar Petrels and 1 Storm Petrel, blown in by recent gales.

DOWNHAM MARKET GAZETTE November 22nd 1879

WHO KILLED COCK ROBIN — *At a taxidermist's shop in East Anglia, the writer observed some half-dozen dead robins: he was told they were being stuffed for ladies' hats. He was further informed that the bird-stuffer had received an order from a London firm for a hundred robins to be used for the same purpose. The birds were killed by small boys with catapults, at a few pence per head.*

EAST ANGLIAN DAILY TIMES January 3rd 1891

Monday, a partridge, perfectly white, was shot at Coddenham. It was sent to Mr. Revett of Brockford who has preserved it as a curiosity.

IPSWICH JOURNAL September 6th 1783

A nest of the Haw Finch has been taken in Ickworth Park containing 5 young ones, now in possession of Mr. Bilson, ornithologist of this town. This makes the fourth nest recorded in this country.

HALESWORTH TIMES June 16th 1857

Give the EASTERN DAILY PRESS their due: in 1894, they were bemoaning the fact that ospreys and egrets were being hunted to extinction to supply plumes to decorate ladies' hats.

Travelling menageries gave the people of East Anglia the opportunity to see exotic animals of which they had only heard exaggerated tales. Escapes by these animals were quite common, as this article shows.

ESCAPE OF AN ELEPHANT — *On Friday evening, Mr. Hylton, owner of the caravans of wild beasts on the Castle meadows, Norwich was showing the elephant to the company; the beast showed signs of insubordination. He was directed to kneel and confess his submission to his keeper, but did not choose to obey, upon which the keeper applied a rather severe punishment . . . The mighty beast just then aimed a tremendous blow at the side of the booth, which at once gave way . . . and the giant of the forest walked off in spite of all opposition, going through the streets, out of St. Stephen's Gates, on to the London Road . . . After about 2 miles' run to Harford Bridges, he sought pleasure or food amongst the umbrageous woods and scanty foliage of Mr. Alderman Thurtell as if enjoying his pristine liberty in his native wilds.*

SUFFOLK CHRONICLE January 25th 1845

The story went on to describe the elephant's recapture, mentioning that complaints had been made about the threat to the public posed by the animals, as *'a lion had already nearly escaped earlier'.*

And finally, two descriptions of hunting that hardly show the pursuit in the best light:

CHASE EXTRAORDINARY — *On Tuesday, the lovers of the chase enjoyed one of the best day's sport ever experienced in this county. Notwithstanding the morning was rather unfavourable, the music of the horn, and the tongue of the hounds, afforded a rich treat to upwards of 100 horsemen and a great number of pedestrians, who met about 10 o'clock on Tannington Green, when a bag fox was turned off before the Framlingham Harriers. He went off in the most gallant style, amidst the cheerings and hallooings of the numerous spectators taking a north-west direction towards Hoxne, passing the covers of Sir Thomas Haselrigg, but as though braving the hounds, he scorned to enter them. The hounds running at a tremendous pace, but few horses were now to be seen with them. He made for Thrandiston turning towards the right for Wortham,* *and having made a short stay in a cover of Admiral Wilson's of Redgrave, still depending on the swiftness of his feet, he ventured on towards Walsham-le-Willows, when every hound took his share of the work with an improved scent, till, at length wearied by the exertions of the day, and completely exhausted, he was descried by the few horsemen who were able to continue the pursuit; and, cheering the high mettled babes, they, with peals of echo and vengeance, soon outstript their devoted prey, and fairly dismembered his exhausted carcass. After a run of 22 miles, with only one check for a few minutes, which was performed in the short space of one hour and forty minutes, six horsemen had the ecstatic felicity of witnessing the glorious termination of the chase. To the astonishment of these gallant riders, the fox, when killed, had only three feet. The other, it is supposed, was lost in a trap in passing through Admiral Wilson's cover.*

SUFFOLK CHRONICLE February 10th 1816

Lately, some gentlemen of distinction were a-fox hunting in Norfolk, and after they had run their fox upwards of 30 miles, he took to a church yard and got into a church through a hole that was under the door, to which the hounds made, and at last jumped through the windows and killed him in the clerk's pew.

NORWICH MERCURY February 1st 1755

From a colour painting by Diana Sperling

12

Sports and wagers

If sport was popular in the eighteenth and early nineteenth centuries, it was not for its own sake. Bets were always a part of any
challenge and even games of cricket, bowls and chess involved a

wager and a prize. The London Chess Club, it was announced in the BURY GAZETTE of February 18th 1824, was to play the Paris club for 50 guineas a game. A game of cricket reported in the IPSWICH JOURNAL of September 10th 1777 between Colchester and Stowmarket, on which much had been placed in wagers, disintegrated into a riot when it became clear that Stowmarket only needed '24 notches' in their second innings to win.

A match at bowls was played upon the Green at Cley next the sea between three gentlemen of Cley and three gentlemen of Holt for 50 guineas a side.

NORFOLK CHRONICLE September 5th 1807

In 1730, the government was looking for ways to raise money, and the national passion for gambling seemed one way to do it. There was already a National Lottery, but they hit on another surefire way to create revenue by taxing the very articles used in gaming.

Tis talked that a duty of 5s. will be laid on every pack of cards, and one guinea upon every pair of dice.

IPSWICH JOURNAL January 24th 1730

Some became rich by such pursuits, though it helped if you had a small fortune to begin with.

Sir Charles Bunbury, it is said, cleared by the last Epsom races, upwards of 1500 guineas.

SUFFOLK CHRONICLE May 30th 1801

A wager of 500 guineas is now depending that one man rides from London to York and back again before another man drives 2 pigs 40 miles on the same road. The pigs are not to have anything tied to their legs or to be in any ways confined, but to walk or run at the direction of the driver.

IPSWICH JOURNAL July 12th 1777

An odd wager is to be decided at the next Newmarket meeting: a gentleman has betted 200 guineas he will ride one horse 30 miles upon the course before a snail can crawl 30 inches on a stone covered with powdered sugar. Great bets are depending on this whimsical wager.

NORFOLK CHRONICLE 1779

Though illegal in public places, games known as Hazard and Faro were popular gambling games of the time. Suffolk papers reported a number of cases brought to court where people were found gambling in public. Publicans were charged with allowing bagatelle and other gambling pursuits to be played on their premises.

A notable practitioner at the game of thimbles and balls was convicted of cheating several persons of their money and received sentence to stand in the pillory and suffer a year's imprisonment.

NORWICH GAZETTE July 24th 1725

EVASION OF LAWS — *The Americans excel in these manoeuvres. An Act was passed to prohibit the playing at ninepins. As soon as the law was put in force, it was notified everywhere 'Ten-pins played here', and they have been played everywhere ever since.*

DISS EXPRESS April 24th 1868

Prize-fighting came in a variety of forms. The IPSWICH JOURNAL of October 22nd 1743 described a great fight between the champions of London and of Norwich. Though the bets were strongly on John James, the London man, the fight, held at the Great Booth in Tottenham Court, went the way of the Norfolk Champion, Mr John Slack:

Slack gave James such falls by cross-buttocks as quite demolished him and his blows with his hands were such as James shrunk at every time. In short, Mr. James was within eight minutes time, by several men, carried off the stage for dead.

This picture shows Slack winning another of his many victories. He was the same John Slack who twice beat Daniel Smith, the Suffolk Champion, at Framlingham in 1744
(see Pip and Joy Wright, Newspapers in Suffolk *vol. 1)*

The IRIS of April 16th 1803 reported a prize-fight that had taken place between Belcher and Firby, alias 'The Young Ruffian'. Sporting gentlemen at Newmarket had raised a subscription, but authorities in Suffolk and Cambridgeshire had taken pains to prevent the fight from taking place. It was held eventually at Linton, where Belcher gave his young opponent a good beating, in a bout that lasted about 20 minutes.

A severe trial of manhood was fought at Ranworth . . . for a considerable sum of money between the noted Watson and one Driver. They fought for upwards of an hour, neither being the victor. Driver is since dead of the bruises he received.
NORWICH MERCURY April 17th 1773

The SUFFOLK CHRONICLE regularly reported boxing fights for large sums of money which drew sizeable crowds, none more so than the following report from 1817.

A match had been made for Sutton and Painter to fight for a purse of 100 guineas somewhere within fifteen miles of Norwich. It became generally known that Bungay Common was the intended scene of action. On Tuesday, long 'ere the early cock had thrice done salutation to the morn, the various roads leading to that town began to be thronged with vehicles of every description; but particularly that between Bungay and Norwich exhibited such a piebald congregation of horse and foot, as has rarely been witnessed on any similar occasion. Stage-coaches and caravans, whiskies and wagons tandems and taxed carts, sociables and sulkies, horses and pedestrians resolutely padded the hoof through the mud and braved the pitiless pelting of the rain. The company amounted to fifteen thousand persons . . . who believed that prize fighting, bull baiting and other old English sports is essential to keep alive that spirit and intrepidity which achieved the glories of Trafalgar and Waterloo.

Sutton, who is a man of colour, on stripping, exhibited a mould truly herculean. Painter, having untogged, displayed a well built frame, but possessing more delicacy than his opponent. In the first round, both men were so cautious that eleven minutes elapsed before a blow was struck, neither seeming inclined to give away the least chance. The fight lasted an hour and forty four minutes, in which time only fifteen rounds were fought.

On the road to see a prize-fight

Painter waited upon 'blackee' and whenever an opportunity offered, he pinked him like a harlequin. Several times he got into his length and punished him about his bread magazine most terribly. He however received a blow on his left listener which would have taken all the fight out of any commoner but he never lost his gaiety and he floored poor Sutton several times in a workman like style.

SUFFOLK CHRONICLE December 20th 1817

The spirit of gambling has arisen to such a height that at a certain chocolate house in St. James Street, two distinguished noblemen, celebrated upon the turf, pitted their wives one against the other for 5,000L.

IPSWICH JOURNAL June 27th 1778

Gaming in public-houses had risen to such a state that the game of bagatelle was banned from pubs in 1841. For the true gentleman, undertaking wagers was almost a full-time occupation.

Last week, Captain Clowes of Ramsgate undertook for a wager, to get out of bed, dress himself and ride a mile . . . which he performed in four minutes and seven seconds. Bets were starting at 100 guineas to 10 against the performance.

IPSWICH JOURNAL November 1816

On Monday last, Mr. Andrew Reed, our city gladiator, who for several years has defeated all swordsmen that have fought him, set out for London to try his skill with the famous Mr. Figg who is thought to have no equal in that science.

NORWICH GAZETTE May 14th 1726

Captain Barclay is at this time engaged in an extraordinary wager – he is begging in Scotland for six weeks, on a wager of 6,000L to subsist as a common beggar on what is given to him and to sleep in a barn &c.

IPSWICH JOURNAL March 18th 1820

A novel game of cricket was played for a considerable sum on Monday on Harefield Common near Rickmansworth, between two gentlemen of Middlesex and Mr. Francis Trumper, farmer of Harefield, with the help of a thorough-bred sheepdog. Mr. Trumper, we were told, won the wager by scoring more runs than the two gentlemen. The match having been talked of in the neighbourhood for weeks, there was a tremendous attendance of spectators, who were amazed at the dog's dexterity. The dog always stood near his master when he was going to bowl, and the moment the ball was hit, he kept his eye upon it and started off after it with speed; and on his master running up to the wicket, the dog would carry the ball in his mouth and put it into his master's hand with such wonderful quickness that the gentlemen found it very difficult to get a run, even from a very long hit.

IPSWICH JOURNAL June 27th 1827

But, of course there were all kinds of people willing to undertake almost any challenge if the money was right.

On Friday last, Mr. Henry Alban of Glemsford, for a considerable wager, picked up 100 eggs, one at a time, placed at the distance of one yard from egg to egg and put them in a basket placed at the end of the hundred yards. He was allowed an hour to do it, but did it in 48 min. without breaking an egg.

IPSWICH JOURNAL October 11th 1777

The IPSWICH JOURNAL for May 1778 described a wager between John Moore, merchant, and Abraham Sherman, butcher, both of Ipswich. Moore claimed his horse would draw a two-ton weight from the Falcon at Ipswich to the Rose and Crown at Colchester, a distance of 17 miles, in just 16 hours. The wager was set for 40 guineas. Large crowds of spectators turned out to see the task which was accomplished in 15 hours 36 minutes. According to the newspaper, Edward Moore, watchmaker and goldsmith, designed the 'machine' drawn by the horse and later sold engravings which pictured the contest.

CAMBRIDGE — *A few days ago, a man for a wager of 10 guineas walked from Halifax to Hepton bridge, which is seven miles and a half, tied up in a sack. He was allowed eleven hours and performed it in six hours and a half.*

IPSWICH JOURNAL March 22nd 1777

On Tuesday morning, at 9, Nicholas Holman, a coal heaver, about 60 years of age, set out from St. Stephen's Gates to carry 6 stone weight of coals from this city to London in 57 hours for a wager of ten guineas. It is said he was at Larlingford (22 miles from Norwich) at 3 o'clock in the afternoon, which was the first place he stopped at. He continued his journey within four miles of Barton Mills, where he thought proper to give up and went no further.

NORWICH MERCURY September 28th 1771

A wager was made between two persons living in the neighbourhood of Cockermouth for 2s. 6d., one of whom swallowed (and by fair mastication) 36 salt herrings, and drank 3 pecks of ale, [a peck = 2 gallons] Winchester measure, within the space of an hour. The cook, being a humourist, fried the last moiety of the herrings in half a pound of candles.

IPSWICH JOURNAL December 31st 1803

The IPSWICH JOURNAL for August 7th 1824 included the story of a bet involving a donkey. Mr Wilson, an Ipswich clothier said for £15 his donkey would pull him in a chaise from the Wagon and Horses in Ipswich to London and back in 48 hours. The description of the journey, which is quite lengthy, mentions all the stopping points along the way and the fact that donkey as well as master were regularly refreshed with old beer and gin and water. They performed the journey with over two hours to spare.

WALKING MATCH — *On Wednesday, a young man named Cooper undertook to walk two miles in 20 minutes, carrying on his head a half-hundredweight and in each hand a plate. The match came off on the Caister Road in the presence of a large number of people. Cooper lost by 25 seconds.*

YARMOUTH GAZETTE January 23rd 1875

The following note, seen in a blacksmith's shop in 1793, was copied and published years later.

This is to give notes that thar is to be a dvarchen as same as eushel at Hunnington on wissen tuesday a nas race and gluvs to be runned for by yung min and buckles to be bouled for, and a chap runned for by young wimmen, and a dance - all you yung min and wimmin shold be welkim at my hous hunnington fox i ham yure umbel sarvent.

BURY AND NORWICH POST August 9th 1826

FEAT EXTRAORDINARY — *On Thursday se'nnight, a gentleman of this university (Cambridge) backed himself against time to perform the following feats — kill twelve pigeons, jump over six hurdles on foot and leap a horse over six more, scull one mile and run one mile in the space of half an hour. He accomplished this in 22 minutes and a half, winning just five pounds.*

IPSWICH JOURNAL March 7th 1840

THE 'SUFFOLK WONDER' — *On Tuesday last a great number of people assembled at Whitton to witness the extraordinary pedestrian feat, by Swift, the 'Suffolk Wonder,' who, as it has been stated, for a wager of twenty sovereigns, engaged to pick up one hundred stones, placed one yard apart, and bring each back to the starting post, and walk two miles, all within the hour. The 'Suffolk Wonder' won his wager with two minutes to spare. We understand that a short time since, Swift walked seven miles in fifty-six minutes.*

IPSWICH JOURNAL December 30th 1843

Some attempts could be foolhardy, or even downright danger-ous, and probably would never have been attempted without the encouragement of a few pints of ale.

Two or three people were drinking one day last week at the Angel Inn at Spalding in Lincolnshire, when one of the company, for a trifling bet, offered to carry a red hot poker in his teeth as far as the obelisk in the market-place, there and back again. The bet being agreed to, the man took the poker between his teeth and performed it. The consequence was, the poor man was so affected that his teeth dropped out, his mouth and his throat was so scorched that he languished till the next day and expired in great agonies.

IPSWICH JOURNAL June 12th 1784

We are almost afraid of telling the story, but it is nevertheless a posi-tive fact that on Saturday night last, at the Dog and Partridge in this town, a man devoured the whole of an earthenware pint mug, except the handle, and would have swallowed that also, but that the person with whom he had betted a trifling wager, expressed himself perfectly satisfied. Of what materials his throat and bowels are composed we know not.

BURY & NORWICH POST
March 15th 1826

A considerable person, not far from St. James' being much addicted to gaming, by which he impoverished his family, finding he had no luck at it, made a rash wish, which was that if ever he played again, his arm might rot off. In a little time he relapsed, and very shortly after, an inflammation fell upon his arm, and notwithstanding

The Dog and Partridge, Bury St Edmunds

all proper means were used to heal it, it turned into a mortification, and killed him.

SUFFOLK MERCURY June 26th 1721

On Monday, two young gentlemen on a wager endeavoured to outdrink each other with Cherry Brandy and one of them who had drunk near 3 quarts was suddenly taken ill and died yesterday at his lodgings. The other is so bad that there is little hope of his recovery.

NORWICH MERCURY September 7th 1751

Wagers over contests of the most traditional kinds could lead to bad feeling. When the bell-ringers of Eye met the bell-ringers of Norwich at Bungay in 1729, they were unable even to agree on the rules of the competition they had intended to embark upon, so a series of advertisements rapidly followed, with each team accusing the other of lying, being unreasonable and avoiding any true competition. Eye put their case first in a reasonably polite 300- word advert on October 18th 1729. This was quickly followed by this (which is but part of a 500-word response):

The Eye ringers (by their lying advertisement concerning the meeting at Bungay) have made it a truth equal to an axiom that impudence and ignorance are inseparable companions; for they would bear the world in hand that we refused to ingage them either at ringing or picking . . . and after they had denied everything, and rung a blundering peal or two, the 'heroes' packed up their bundle of conceit and sneaked out of town in the dark, wisely preventing being hissed at by the people . . . So we leave them to be judged by all men of sound reason and now clear our hands of them as unworthy of our further notice.

NORWICH GAZETTE October 25th 1729

But the ringers of Eye were not going to take that without reply. This was just a taste of their advert that, this time, ran to over a thousand words.

Forasmuch as the Norwich Society of Ringers have, in their late scurrilous advertisement, falsely and maliciously aspersed the EYE RINGERS with a misrepresentation of the proposals that were introduced at the Bungay meeting, and have very genteely given us the lie, designing thereby to bring an odium upon our characters: We . . . think it justly deserves our highest resentment, lest the world should be imposed upon to believe the scandalous and no less infamous suggestions of a parcel of ra—ls, whose insolence and arrogance . . . false and groundless . . . void of truth and good manners . . . whose ringing was so odious, that all the little petty ringers of the country towns adjacent hissed at their performances . . .

NORWICH GAZETTE November 8th 1729

Yes, I think we get the gist of it. And then, of course, things could get completely out of hand:

SILLY SUFFOLK — *Bills having been posted in Ipswich intimating that a Mr. E. J. Maitland of Worcester, would, on Tuesday afternoon at 2 o'clock, do what nobody else had dreamed of achieving — walk upon the water from Stoke Bridge to the Griffin and back by means of an easy* *and simple plan of his own, several thousands found their way to the spot, anxious to see the marvellous performance. Not only were the banks of the river lined with spectators, but the tops of houses, the ends of cranes, the rigging of the ships in the dock, were all made use of: most of the skiffs were also brought into requisition – in short, every available spot and thing was appropriated, and an expectant public waited with a good deal of patience till late in the afternoon, when, waking up to the hoax of which they had been the victims, the majority left, some of them taking a circuitous route home to avoid the good-natured chaff which now and then saluted the unlucky dupes. The hoax originated, as we have been given to understand, in a bet made by a gentleman that he would draw a given number to the water side, and he resorted to the 'walking on the water' lie to deceive the people.*

SUFFOLK CHRONICLE October 22nd 1859

The EASTERN DAILY PRESS recounts the tale of a man entering a railway carriage in which the only other passenger was a young lady:

Sitting down beside her, he took from his bag a knife and a turnip, which he peeled before remarking coolly, 'I hope you like raw turnip because you are going to eat this one.' So saying, he cut off a slice and offered it to her. Believing him to be mad, and quite alive to the formidable size of the knife, the unfortunate girl was compelled to swallow the uninviting vegetable. He then threw knife and turnip out of the window and molested her no further. When the train stopped at the station, the 'lunatic' jumped out and gaily greeted a friend, 'All right, I've won my bet.' The train moved on and she considered it the better part to let the matter pass over quietly.

EASTERN DAILY PRESS
July 7th 1894

13
War and the wider world

For much of the eighteenth and nineteenth centuries, Britain was at war with somebody. Towards the end of 1745, reports focused on 'Scotch Affairs', as the Young Pretender moved southwards in spite of reports of provisions of men, cannon, shovels and axes and 'tin-boats' being sent north. Also, local papers carried stories of the depredations of the enemy on the countryside and people of the North of England. Tales of woe were printed from Derby, Coventry, Stafford and Lichfield. Bonny Prince Charlie was uncomfortably close. Despite that, the local press come across as being remarkably calm about the whole business. The NORWICH MERCURY announced that King's Lynn had raised 600 men in the town's defence, and Cambridge alone had amassed a fighting fund of over £4,000. After the decisive battle, close to Northampton, the retreating Scots were pursued mercilessly by the victorious English soldiers. Reports over the following three years would appear, recounting the trials of those administrators north of the border who had 'allowed matters to get that far.'

The gung-ho attitude of soldiers writing home from the front has changed little over the last 200 years. The BURY POST in August 1855 published a letter sent by a soldier to his mother in reply to a letter she had sent him, upbraiding him for not writing to her.

Barracks, Scutari. – Dear Mother, you really must excuse me for not sending you a letter before . . . I am now living in a tent with thirteen others and the flies are so numerous I can scarcely see two yards before me. I am sorry to tell you, I fell down a cliff last Monday and broke one of the bones in my left arm: It is very painful, but is, I hope, going on well. I need not tell you that owing to this I have no duty to perform, and really think it an interposition of providence; for I was literally worn out in the cholera wards, which, I am happy to say, are now nearly empty. We are ordered to go to the front next month, when I shall be quite in my element. With kindest and best love to all, I remain your affectionate son, William.

> *Don't be angry, mother, mother,*
> *Let your smiles be smiles of joy;*
> *Don't be angry, mother, mother,*
> *Don't be angry with your boy.*

Months have pass'd since we were parted,
I have travelled o'er the sea;
And your boy, near brokenhearted
Ne'er has ceased to think of thee.

Many a night both wet and weary,
I have sat and thought of thee,
In those trenches damp and gory:
Thou hast also thought of me.

And then there were the spoils of war. The IPSWICH JOURNAL for
April 7th 1804 announced an auction of goods at Great Yarmouth,
including 13,410 Edam cheeses, 924 Gouda cheeses, 166 casks of
butter, with large quantities of timber and corn. All this had been
captured from Dutch ships in the North Sea.

Even as long ago as 1809, the press emphasized the pride felt
regarding the war effort and the humane way we treated our prisoners of war.

As a striking contrast of the treatment experienced by the prisoners of
war in this country and France, we need only to mention that the bag-
gage belonging to the prisoners of the Bienfaisant, *lately removed from*
Plymouth to Dartmoor, exclusive of what they carried with them, filled 35
carts – while our countrymen, prisoners in that country, are not allowed
to possess any property other than the clothes they wear.

IPSWICH JOURNAL June 3rd 1809

A most beautiful and noble sight presented itself at Aldborough on
Thursday. It consisted of upwards of 350 ships, many from the Baltic,
laden with timber, deals and naval stores, colliers and some from
Flushing with French prisoners and wounded men. What wind there
was being against them, at the turn of the tide, they anchored off that
place and remained within a small distance the greater part of the day.
What a proud and gratifying sight for Old England. Such a one as the
oldest inhabitant there does not remember to have seen before.

IPSWICH JOURNAL August 26th 1809

Of course, not every-one involved in conflict wanted to be there. The IPSWICH JOURNAL for March 24th 1804 advertised a reward for the capture of Robert Simmons, who had *'absconded from the parish of Blythburgh having been balloted for the Old Militia'.* Being required to belong to the Napoleonic equiv-alent of the Home Guard was one thing, but join-ing the real armed forces was another.

COLCHESTER — *The press gang that was down here, and in the neigh-bourhood, after having picked up several idle hands is returned to London.*
IPSWICH JOURNAL March 8th 1777

Thursday night there was a very hot press on the River Thames. They paid no regard to protections, but stripped every vessel of all their hands that were useful. They boarded the Glatton, East-Indiaman; but the crew made a stout defence, got on shore, and came into London about 12 o'clock last night. It is computed that on the river and on shore, they took upwards of 700.
NORWICH MERCURY January 5th 1771

In my book *Death Recorded* are cases from Ipswich and Norwich (1779 and 1882) where the over-enthusiasm of the press-gangs and recruiting sergeants led to death and serious injury. People would do almost anything to avoid being conscripted.

A General Court Martial assembled on Tuesday at the Military Depot at Stowmarket for the trial of a boy lately enlisted into the 12th Regt. of Foot for wilfully cutting off his finger, under an idea of incapacitating himself for a soldier.

IPSWICH JOURNAL September 29th 1810

At times, large numbers of soldiers were encamped around this region, training and awaiting embarkation for the continent. Much of the crime reported was down to these soldiers, including a number of murders in the early 1800s. As long ago as 1766, the NORWICH MERCURY was reporting the hanging of a soldier named John Ruderham at Lynn for the murder of Leonard Wilson. In his last speech, he was reported as saying '*his ruin commenced from his entering into the service of the Essex Militia*'. Anti-social behaviour was not restricted to the lower ranks. Officers regularly fell out over matters of honour and had their own very special way of handling it.

Tuesday morning last, we understand, an affair of honour was settled beween Captains R——n and G——t of the Militia in garrison. The parties met West of the Horse Barracks; the first fire was tossed up for, and a brace of pistols discharged without effect. The seconds interferred to no purpose, and another brace were resorted to and used without any other effect than slightly grazing the leg of the former. On the seconds again interferring, the affair was honourably terminated. The cause of the misunderstanding we are not acquainted with.

NORFOLK CHRONICLE March 29th 1806

The same column reported another duel fought on Galleywood Common near Chelmsford where Mr Fisher, surgeon to the 6th regiment of foot, killed Lieut. Torrens in a duel before absconding. One of the seconds, we were told, was under arrest. Duelling was illegal but popular, giving rise to debates in the Commons in March 1844. The LYNN ADVERTISER recounted that over the previous 70 years 200 duels had been fought, in which over 80 had been killed (in three cases, both participants). There had been 20 trials as a result, and four had been found guilty of murder, two of whom had hanged. The names of the duellists had included Dukes of York, Norfolk, Bedford and Buckingham.

The effects of war on the region, both during the hostilities and afterwards, could be significant. We still have the Martello Towers to remind us of less peaceful times. Also,

> *An inclosure of brick-work, fourteen feet high, and of the vast circumference of nearly a mile is building round the prison at Norman Cross to prevent the escape of the foreign prisoners confined there, whose attempts to procure their liberty have lately been numerous and daring. Some nights ago, between ten and eleven o'clock, a party of them, 500 in number, endeavoured to break out . . . they were charged by the military of the barracks and more than 40 severely wounded before they were driven back. None of them escaped.*
>
> NORFOLK CHRONICLE October 3rd 1807

> *The parish of Rushford raised £15-11-6 for the Balaclava Fund, thus saving survivors from the Charge of the Light Brigade from the Workhouse and paupers' graves.*
>
> THETFORD WEEKLY POST December 15th 1905

Neighbouring countries, across the channel in Europe, more often than not, were mocked by our local newspaper correspondents. These stories were typical of many written at the time of the Crimean War.

A French soldier at Sebastopol wrote to his father, asking him to send a pair of shoes and a five-franc piece. His father, not sure how to send them, hung the new shoes, with the coin inside, on the telegraph wires, assuming they would be transmitted there. Soon after, a mason returning home, spotted the shoes on the wires, found they fitted his feet and pocketed the five-franc piece. He left his own threadbare shoes in their place. When the father returned, he said happily, 'not only has my boy received his new shoes, he has returned his old ones.'

WEST SUFFOLK & NORTH ESSEX FREE PRESS
September 27th 1855

A duel was recently fought between an Englishman and a Russian in a darkened room . . . The Englishman, not wishing to have blood on his hands, fired his pistol up the chimney, and, to his horror, down came the Russian.

BURY FREE PRESS July 28th 1855

It was easy to laugh at foreigners. America was a constant source of comic tales. In one told by the SWAFFHAM JOURNAL, a hotel owner entered a room to discover the man who had been employed to wash the windows reading a newspaper.

Being an active man himself, he had no use for a lazy man [and] discharged the washer on the spot and ordered him to go to the office for his pay. The sacked man changed out of his work-clothes into his Sunday best and went to pick up his money. On leaving, he encountered the hotel owner again, but was not recognised, so different did he look.

'Here my man,' said the hotel owner, 'You look as if you have some good work in you – do you want a job? Can you wash windows? I have just discharged a man who has been doing that sort of work. I paid him only 20 dollars a month, but if you will take the place and go right to work, I'll pay you 22 dollars.'

The proposition was quickly accepted, and in half an hour the dis-

charged employee was scrubbing away in the same old room.
                    SWAFFHAM JOURNAL January 25th 1879

In the STOWMARKET COURIER in May 1890, we learn that the champion egg-eater of the world was an American, having eaten 200 eggs in under 2 minutes. And just to prove Irish jokes are nothing new:

A conceited coxcomb with a very patronising air called out to an Irish labourer, 'Here, you bog-trotter, come and tell me the greatest lie you can, and I will treat you to a glass of whiskey.' 'By my word,' said Pat, 'an', yer honour's a gentleman.'
                    DISS EXPRESS April 24th 1868

Distant and exotic locations were literally a world away to most of the readers who were prepared to believe and enjoy exaggerated details of life elsewhere. The IRIS of April 2nd 1803 described a statement published at St Petersburg, saying they had 12 persons of 120 years of age, two persons aged 121, one aged 124, two aged 125, two aged 128 and four aged 138. The HUNSTANTON TELEPHONE of August 17th 1878 reported the oldest man in the world as being a Miguel Solis of Colombia, aged 180 years.

Letters from Lisbon give an account of three monstrous births which lately happened there, the like of which perhaps was never heard of. The first was a beautiful young lady, rich, and the only child of her parents, who suffered a large water-dog to lye with her, by which she conceived and was delivered of three monsters which had shoulders, claws and head like a dog, and from the middle downward like a man. Another woman was also delivered of three monsters, two dead and one alive, their heads and the fore-parts of their bodies like monkeys with a long bushy tail. That which came alive was stifled in a pan of hot water, their pictures were drawn and set up to publick view. A third woman was delivered of a dead child, whose back was gnawed by five serpents, which came alive into the world with it and leapt up and down the room, which so frightened the midwife and others present as made them run out, but the husband took courage and entered the room with a stick and destroyed them.
                    [Norwich] WEEKLY MERCURY OR PROTESTANT PACKET
                    October 20th 1722

SHAH'S HAREM — *Despatches from Baku disclose what, in Persian circles, are regarded as most dangerous unsuspected revolutionary tendencies in the Shah. He has just reduced the number of his Harem from 1,700 to 60. It smacks of the West and sacrilege, and it is feared that the antiforeign subjects of His Majesty may rise up in rebellion against him. No Shah ever had less than 1,500 wives, and when the present Shah ascended the throne, his father's legacy included 1,600 wives and several hundred children. The Shah's act in reducing his harem to an unheard-of number is looked upon as the most astounding innovation ever accomplished.*

WOODBRIDGE REPORTER December 11th 1902

STRANGE ATTEMPT AT POISONING — *An attempt at poisoning lately took place at Marges, a small village in the Drome, under singular circumstances. The wife of a carpenter, whose moral habits were not of the strictest kind, conceived the idea of getting rid of her husband in* *order that she might with less restraint carry on an illicit connection with another man with whom she was known to be connected. For this purpose, she went to an apothecary at Romans and asked for some arsenic to kill the rats with which her house, she said, was swarming. The apothecary refused, saying he could only deliver arsenic to her husband in the presence of witnesses. A few days after, the husband happened to come to the shop for some article, when he was asked whether the rats still disturbed him. 'I have never heard any,' was the reply. He was told what the wife had done, when he said: 'Ah, the coquine, she wants to poison me.' It was then agreed that if she came again, the apothecary should give her some harmless substance, and when the husband had eaten his dinner, he should fall down and pretend to be dead. The farce was carried on as arranged. The wife, to make the world believe that death was the result of suicide, took a rope, and making a running knot, passed it round the neck of her husband and then went into an upper room to the beam of which she had fastened the end of the rope, in order to pull him up. The moment she left, the husband slipped off the rope from his neck and tied it to a bench. The woman began to pull, but finding the body heavier than she expected, she came down again to see what prevented her lifting him. Her husband gave her some hearty blows and afterwards had her carried to prison.*

NORFOLK NEWS February 5th 1853

A BEAN COLLECTOR — *An eccentric individual has just died in Paris . . . The great fancy of his life was to collect beans. He had beans from all the countries in the world, carefully ticketed and arranged. Only a few days ago he paid 100 francs apiece for 5 beans from China. His old housekeeper seems of the opinion that his death was accelerated from the intense grief he had lately experienced in consequence of having missed from his collection ten peculiar beans from Japan. He left a voluminous manuscript 'The Natural History of Haricots' and he also wrote some lengthy poems in praise of beans.*

BURY FREE PRESS January 12th 1867

14

Superstition

Trying to explain the inexplicable continues to test the imaginations of copy-writers to this day. It was always so. The BURY AND NORWICH POST of April 12th 1826 reported a strange case of 'Corpus sant' on Cromer church tower. What appears to have been a case of St Elmo's fire (an electrical discharge, often associated with thunderstorms) was described as 'like the lights often seen on ships' masts'. The report went on to suggest possible reasons for such a phenomenon were glowing insects or the raising of a substance from the surface of the ocean by the wind.

Stories involving superstitious belief can be divided into a number of categories. Take, for example, monsters.

Captain Woodward and the mate and seamen of the schooner Adamant, which arrived at Hingham on Sunday last, saw about twelve leagues east of Cape Ann a sea serpent, apparently upwards of 100 feet long, which frequently raised its head a considerable height above the water. It was very near the vessel for about five hours, a full view was had of it and it appeared to be about as large round as a barrel. It was once fired at and appeared irritated by the explosion.

SUFFOLK CHRONICLE June 27th 1818

WROXHAM – THE HUGE SNAKE – *We have been favoured by a yachting friend with an account of this monster, which was noticed at Herringfleet, about a fortnight ago, and he informs us it has been seen at Wroxham, having evidently made its way thither by the North River via Yarmouth. When our friend first saw it, it was making its way at a furious rate towards the mouth of the North River. At first he thought it was a shark, but on firing a double shot at it, it reared its horrible head out of the water higher than his topmast, hissing and roaring fearfully, while its tail lashed the water into foam for several fathoms. He computed the length to be about 80 feet or a little more, judging from the length of the yacht. The colour was a dull yellow, spotted with black, the eyes were small but fiery . . . the back of the neck was covered with a shaggy substance like seaweed, and*

its sides armour-plated with watery hideous looking scales . . . Following on up the river, he was fortunate enough to get another sight of it, apparently in deadly encounter with a gigantic pike, which it ultimately swallowed and disappeared, evidently going to the bottom to gorge and enjoy its meal.

This picture appeared in a 1721 issue of the NORTHAMPTON MERCURY, *to accompany a news item rather like the one on this page.*

DISS EXPRESS
September 25th
1874

Following a letter to the IPSWICH JOURNAL in May 1721 inquiring about mermaids, a remarkable article was published.

Some think 'em not be creatures as such, but monsters got by unnatural copulation; some think 'em to be devils; some say that when the angels fell, those that fell in the sea were turned into mermen; some say that devils begat them of fishes; some that fishes generating in the Deluge [Noah's flood] and seeing drowned men, by strength of imagination got something like them. In our English chronicles 'tis affirmed a man-fish was taken at Orford in this county of Suffolk, kept six months on shore and stole again to sea. But the most authentic story we meet with is in the history of the Netherlands. The dykes were broken down by an inundation in 1403 and a merwoman was left in Dermert Mere . . . The milkmaids who used to cross the mere, used her kindly and cleaned the sea moss and shells from off her and offered her water, fish, milk and bread, which she refused, but in a day or two, they got her to eat and drink. Her hair was long and black, her face human, her teeth very strong, her breasts and belly to her navel were perfect; the lower parts of her body ended in a strong fish tail. The magistrates of Harlem commanded her to be brought thither and put into the town house . . .

She learnt to spin and show devotion at prayer . . . though she could never be taught to speak. She would wear no clothes in summer. She would have her tail in the water and accordingly had a tub of water under her chair made on purpose for her. She lived thus for fifteen or sixteen years and when she died, she was buried in the churchyard. Her picture was painted on a board with oil and hangs now in the town house of Harlem.

IPSWICH JOURNAL May 1721

Then of course, we have ghosts and apparitions.

THE SYDERSTONE GHOST — *This mystery is not yet solved and the disturbances are more annoying than ever. On Wednesday week, Mr. Stewart requested several most respectable gentlemen to sit up all night with him (these included three ministers of the church and a local surgeon). Especial care was taken that no tricks should be played by the servants; but as if to give the visitors a grand treat, the noises were even louder and* *of longer contin-uance than usual. The first com-mencement was in the bed-chamber of Miss Stewart, and seemed like the clawing of a voracious animal after its prey. The effect on all present was like a shock of electric-ity, but nothing was visible . . . The disturber was conjured to speak but answered only by a low hollow moan-ing; on being*

requested to give three knocks, it gave three most tremendous blows some of which were as loud as those of a hammer on an anvil. The following is the account given by one of the gentlemen:- 'We all heard distinct sounds of various kinds, from various parts of the room and the air; we felt the vibrations of parts of the bed, but we were quite unable to assign any pos-sible natural cause as producing all or any part of this. We all left equally bewildered.' Few nights pass away without such visitations, and each one brings its own variety.

SUFFOLK CHRONICLE June 1st 1833

The ghost which haunted Syderstone Rectory was supposed to have belonged to Amy Robsart, wife of Robert Dudley, Earl of Leicester, whose mysterious death in 1560 led to the suspicion that she had been murdered to enable her husband to marry Elizabeth I.

Although the hall where she had lived had been demolished, the nearby rectory suffered from a large amount of poltergeist activity.

The YARMOUTH INDEPENDENT described in May 1894 how a farmhouse at Blofield had suffered mysterious ghostly visitations.

> *Sometimes an old man appeared, sometimes an old woman, candles went out and strange noises were heard, to such an extent servants refused to dwell there.*

People write letters to the editors of papers for all sorts of reasons. It may be because they have an opinion about something that they want to see published. Sometimes, however, letters are written because people want to share an unusual experience they have had with the readers of their favourite paper. On March 1st 1834, Major Edward Moor of Great Bealings House, near Woodbridge, had a long letter published in the IPSWICH JOURNAL describing a lot of unexplained ghostly activity in his house. Large houses with a lot of servants had a system of bells that could be rung to call maids to any part of the house. At Bealings, the bells had begun to ring of their own accord so that sometimes all the bells in the house were ringing violently together. Major Moor described how the system had been checked and the wires replaced. In response to any suggestion that it might have been a trick he wrote,

> *I have for many years of my life passed over large areas of the earth's surface and have seen divers tricks of distant people. If this be one, it surpasses all that I have seen.*

Our local newspapers liked nothing more than uncovering hoaxes and demonstrating just how gullible East Anglians could be.

> **LAVENHAM** — *A most singular annoyance commenced at Mrs. East's of the Blackbird Public House in this town, which has continued, at intervals up to this day. Scarcely a whole pane is left in any of the windows at the back of the house and very few have escaped in front . . . Many a grandmother's marvellous tale has been adduced to prove that this has been occasioned by WITCHES AND WIZARDS. It has to be hoped that*

the activity of the officers, and the reward which is offered, will in a short time bring the 'hobgoblins' to the seat of justice.

SUFFOLK CHRONICLE May 17th 1823

ANOTHER GHOST! — *The inhabitants of Cox Lane, in this town, have been thrown into a state of consternation at the appearance of a ghost or ghosts, assuming the awful shapes of a female in white and a gristly bear, with a tremendous pair of jaws and a suitable row of tusks! It appears, that a shoemaker, who had only a day before become the tenant of a house in the lane, which had been for some time shut up, was seated*

on Thursday se'nnight, at work with his journey-man in a chamber, when, between six and seven o'clock in the evening, they were horror-struck at seeing the aforesaid white lady enter the room and before they could recover breath suddenly vanish through the wall! These sons of Crispin quickly scampered out of the house, but fancying their visual organs had deceived them soon returned and recommenced their work. In a short time, however, another form far more formidable in appearance presented itself in the similitude of an enormous bear, which, with distended jaws threatened to swallow them up at a meal. This was too much for human nature to endure, and the occupier and his man made a precipitate retreat, and have taken up their quarters in a more peaceable neighbourhood. The perpetrator of the joke has not yet been discovered.

SUFFOLK CHRONICLE March 25th 1837

CAPTURE OF A GHOST! – *For several nights during the past week, the sentries on duty at Landguard Fort have been alarmed by an apparently supernatural appearance. On Sunday night last this was again observed, and the sentry then on duty, being more courageous than his predecessors, challenged the apparition, and receiving no reply, charged, upon which the ghost (?) fled in a most ignominious manner. The sentry then turned out the guard, a search was at once instituted, and the ghost (?) was found under a bed in the barracks, in a shape of a soldier, with a pillow round his head and enveloped in a sheet. The 'would be ghost,' a private of the 56th regiment, was sent to the camp, Colchester, on Monday, for trial by Court Martial.*
                    IPSWICH & COLCHESTER TIMES February 4th 1859

A goblin which once haunted the Woodbridge Town Common and which had been laid by the Bishop, has reappeared to many at the Rainbow Tavern, where it is hoped a 'prosecution' will banish 'his ghostship' to the churchyard where he belongs.
                    IPSWICH & COLCHESTER TIMES December 31st 1858

And our newspapers loved to mock those stupid enough to be duped.

SUPERSTITION – *About 9 o'clock on Wednesday evening as a cattle dealer of Linton was on his way home from Bury market, near the Cheveley Park corner he was very much frightened at the sudden appearance of a dark figure resembling a man's legs and part of a body which kept four or five yards in advance of him. Having spoken to it and receiving no answer, he became greatly alarmed. The poor man hastened to the porter's lodge at Cheveley Park and related his tale, and from thence he was ultimately escorted to the Cheveley Star public house, where he continued for the night. On the following night, a person who suspected the cause of this unsightly apparition, resolved to ascertain whether such a thing was really to be seen on that road or not. He waited for the rising of the moon, and just as she had risen above the horizon, the same figure did really appear, which according to everyone's expectation proved to be his own shadow.*
                    SUFFOLK CHRONICLE February 9th 1850

John Kiniman, a poor shoemaker of Nisby was, by upwards of a thousand spectators (very near relations to the wise men of Gotham) from all the neighbouring villages, conducted to a great pond in Kelmarsh Lordship, and underwent the discipline of the ducking stool, for being suspected as a wizard, and conspiring with the Devil, his master, to prevent the lazy dairy women's making good butter and cheese &c. There was also one Barwick, who, in his great integrity to see justice done, offered himself to (and did) take the same diversion, in order to prove that the wizard could not be plunged under water so soon and easy as himself, tho' it is said, that another dipping would have brought many of the undertakers of this political way of trying wizards and witches to have made but an indifferent figure at our ensuing Assizes, as was the fate of some of their neighbouring country folks a few years since, when a poor old woman lost her life.

IPSWICH GAZETTE July 5th 1735

The SUFFOLK GAZETTE for March 6th 1736 reported that a bill had been carried through Parliament, repealing the acts against witch-craft that still stood on the statute books. The NORWICH MERCURY of April 1751 demonstrated that large numbers still believed in witches and were on the side of anyone standing up to them. Thomas Colley of Tring was the only one of six to be found guilty of murder. It was proved he killed one Ruth Osborne, believing her to be a witch. '*It proved impossible to hang him* [and gibbet him, as intended] a*s the people were determined to rescue him, believing that he had behaved reasonably and that she was a witch and a sorceress.*' Other more local cases involving witchcraft can be read in my book *Witches in and around Suffolk.*

In Hoo in Suffolk,

A farmer by the name of Fenner lost a considerable quantity of poultry by a distemper with which they were seized; and having some time before their mortality received a present of a duck from a friend, it was sup-posed from her laying dun-coloured eggs that she had been bewitched by an elderly woman in the neighbourhood, and that was the cause of the losses sustained. In order to prevent a recurrence of similar disasters and to break the enchantment, it was determined by an ignorant and superstitious female servant to burn the ill-fated but innocent victim alive, which horrid resolution she has carried into practice by putting the poor animal into an oven and burning a faggot of wood over her . . . In a short period, from her inhuman conduct, this unfortunate dupe of superstition and ignorance was seized with fits, which appears like a just retribu-

tion. She was thus deprived of that life which she was unworthy of, as she survived but a few days after, expiring in the greatest agonies.

IPSWICH JOURNAL January 7th 1809

FORTUNE TELLING *— The wife of a labourer named Stephen Hatch, residing at Little Bromley, was robbed of £8 10s. on Thursday last, by a gipsy who induced the credulous woman to allow her to deposit the treasure in a small box, under pretence of giving her victim a peep into the future.*

WEST SUFFOLK &
NORTH ESSEX FREE PRESS
May 15th 1856

In a similar story a hundred years earlier, the IPSWICH JOURNAL (July 12th 1755) told of the trial of

> *Mary Smith, an old gipsy . . . stealing from a person near Snowhill 24 guineas, at the time persuading him he was to become an excedingly rich man in 3 hours time after her departure from him.*

But the best tales are always those for which there is no rational explanation.

> *A cobbler, who lived in this city (Bristol), having sometimes had words with an old woman in the neighbourhood, would often call her an old witch. In order to be revenged on him, she sent to his house a cat, which catch'd hold of his finger and would not let it go till it was squeezed to death, after which the poor man endured violent pains in his arm and shoulder, and though he was dipped nine times in salt water, he died in the utmost agony.*
>
> IPSWICH JOURNAL November 5th 1743

Following the hanging of Dr Dodd for forgery, the following anecdote was published.

> *Several years ago Dr. Dodd and his wife went on a pleasurable jaunt to Bristol. Whilst they were there, it was usual with them to ride out in the morning for the benefit of the air in the outskirts of the town. In one of these excursions, they met a flock of gypsies, who surrounded them, and begged they might lay open to them the future incidents of their lives. Mrs. Dodd was for complying with their humour, not through any reliance upon their predictions, but merely to divert herself with a little harmless merriment.*

Apparently Mrs Dodd paid them to tell her fortune but the doctor refused.

> *. . . One of the gypsies, bawled out, 'since you won't give us anything I'll tell your fortune for nothing. You seem to carry your head very high now, but it will be raised higher yet before you die, for you will be hanged.'*
>
> *Some time afterwards, the doctor and Mrs. Dodd going together with several others in the packet from Dover to Calais, a violent storm arose,*

A NEW FORTUNE-TELLING BOOK,
By Dr. PARKINS.
Published this day by Tegg, 111, Cheapside, price 2s. 6d.
The UNIVERSAL FORTUNE TELLER.
CONTAINING

Decrees of Fate.	Secret Writing.
Guide to Hidden Secrets.	Wheel of Fortune.
Future Events and Contingencies.	Art of Divination.
	Oracles by Dreams.
Astrology, Physiognomy, Geomancy, Palmestry.	Silent Language.
	Mathematical Magic.
Signs by Planets, Marks and Scars.	Curious Questions, how to know all things. Past,
Moles, Birds, Beasts, &c.	Present and to Come.

☞ The whole is illustrated by curious Wood Cuts,
of Signs, Figures, Planets, &c.
Where may be had,
Dr. Parkins' New Edition of Culpepper's English Herbal, 5s. bound. The same on fine paper with coloured plates, 7s. 6d. boards.

---

*and the passengers were dreadful apprehensions of being cast away. Dr.
Dodd, who thought there was no danger, in order to cheer up the drooping
spirits of the company, very facetiously said, 'you may be assured that no
harm will arise, for, as I am born to be hanged, you cannot be drowned.'*
IPSWICH JOURNAL July 5th 1777

To balance all this superstition, perhaps a small item about faith
might be in order.

*Mr. Heron, a minister, had a large family of children. When dying, his
weeping wife said, 'Alas! What will become of all these children?' He
pleasantly replied, 'Never fear. He that feeds the young ravens surely
won't starve the young Herons.'*
LYNN ADVERTISER February 15th 1842

15
Famous people

Odd stories about the great and famous have cropped up in our local papers from time to time.

Dickens reading to his daughters

Mr. Charles Dickens, it is stated, is overwhelmed with requests for his autograph. He deals with them summarily, however. Applicants receive a printed answer saying, 'to comply with your modest request would not be reasonably possible.' It is said that to envelope, direct and mail these replies, the services of three secretaries are constantly required.
Diss Express January 24th 1868

Henrik Ibsen, the Norwegian author, loves to keep his hair in disorder. This is said to be his one vanity. He always carries a little toilet-case, containing a looking-glass and a comb, which are attached to the lining of his grey hat. He will often remove his hat to see how his hair is lying. If it is not rough enough to suit his fancy, he uses the comb to give it the requisite tangle.

WOODBRIDGE REPORTER December 11th 1902

The death of the composer Gounod was put down to *'a seizure brought on by M. Gounod's pertinacity in over-taxing his brain'* (EASTERN DAILY PRESS October 19th 1893).

Someone like Nelson was always worth a story, even if it was published nearly eighty years after his death.

When Nelson visited the Royal Naval Hospital at Yarmouth after the battle of Copenhagen, he went round the wards and stopping at every bed, to every man said something kind and cheering. At length, he stopped opposite to a bed on which was lying a sailor who had lost his right arm close to the shoulder joint, when the following short dialogue ensued.

'Well Jack, what's the matter with you?'

'Lost my right arm, your honour.'

Nelson paused, looked down at his own empty sleeve, then at the sailor, and said playfully, 'Well Jack, you and I are spoiled for fisherman; cheer up my brave fellow.'

WOODBRIDGE REPORTER August 2nd 1883

What I find most exciting is to read accounts of significant historical events as they were reported at the time. Often, as in this case, for obvious reasons the article first appeared some time after the event.

The contents of the dispatches from Captain Edwards, Commander of His Majesty's ship, Pandora, who was sent out soon after the return of Capt. Bligh from the South Seas, in search of Christian and the other mutineers who ran away with the Bounty armed ship, on the bread-fruit expedition, are, that on the Pandora's appearing off Otaheite, two men swam off from the shore and solicited to be taken on board; they proved to be two of the Bounty's mutineers and immediately gave intelligence where fourteen of their companions were concealed on the island. A part of the Pandora's crew were instantly dispatched in search of them, and after some little resistance they were taken and brought prisoners on board. Christian, with the other nine mutineers, had previously sailed in the Bounty to some remote island, and every exertion of the Pandora to discover their retreat proved ineffectual. On her return home, the Pandora struck upon a reef of rocks in Endeavour's Straits, and had her bottom beat in. Her crew were happily saved, and escaped from their perilous situation to an island in the Straits, except 33 men and three of the Bounty's people who unfortunately perished by the boat oversetting. Christian will doubtless be pursued, by Capt. Bligh, when the Providence reaches the South Seas; as he is in full possession of every particular respecting the desperadoes and as the Bounty is with him, it may possibly lead to his detection.

IPSWICH JOURNAL April 7th 1792

Captain Bligh landing on Timor after 47 days in an open boat

Genuine heroes are few and far between, but when they did appear, the nation took them to their heart. Take for example, this story from 1838. The *Forfarshire* steamboat from Hull to Dundee set out with her boilers already giving cause for concern. As the weather worsened off St Abbs Head, abandoning ship seemed the only option. There was little chance of rescue, and 45 perished, including the captain. However,

> *Three persons were taken off the wreck aboout 9 o'clock by Mr. Darling, keeper of the outer light and his daughter in their small boat at the imminent risk of their lives.*

BURY & NORWICH POST September 19th 1838

Grace Darling and her father, painted by William Bell Scott

The following week, another article condemned ships that endangered life by putting to sea in an unfit state, and announced, *'a subscription has been opened to reward Grace Darling and her father for noble daring'*. Within weeks, these two would become reluctant celebrities, remembered to this day for their selfless courage.

To return to Nelson; our local papers did him proud. His last moments were reported in a detail that very much reflects the way such things were handled two hundred years ago. We have full forensic details of the passage of the ball through his body and the damage it caused, followed by this thorough if doubtful conversation between the dying Nelson and Hardy.

When Captain Hardy entered the cockpit, Lord Nelson told the latter to come near him. Captain Hardy kissed his cheek. 'I hope your Lordship,' he said, 'will still live to enjoy your triumph.' 'Never, Hardy,' he said, 'I am dying, I am a dead man all over; Beatty will tell you so; bring the fleet to an anchor; you have all done your duty; God bless you.' Captain Hardy now said, 'I suppose Collingwood, my dear Lord, is to command the fleet?'

HMS *Victory*

'Never, (exclaimed he) while I live.' His Lordship said to Mr. Beatty while he was expiring in his arms, 'I could have wished to have lived to enjoy this, but God's will be done.' – 'My Lord, (exclaimed Hardy) you die in the midst of triumph.' 'Do I, Hardy?' – He smiled faintly. 'God be praised.' These were his last words.

No procession that has ever taken place in this country will equal, in point of grandeur and pomp, that which will be displayed at the funeral of Lord Nelson.

NORFOLK CHRONICLE January 4th 1806

Which brings us to royalty. Where famous people are concerned, none were more important to newspaper readers than the British royal family. In 1726, we had both an existing royal family and a potential one in exile. The activities of 'The Pretender' were fully reported, as he seemed to lead a more exciting life than an ageing George I, with his feasts and balls, travelling and gaming, and audiences with the Pope.

There are many royal links with East Anglia.

> *Yesterday, the Sheriffs of Norwich presented His Majesty with twelve herring pies, according to annual custom, by which they hold their charter.*
> NORWICH MERCURY October 31st 1737

The SWAFFHAM JOURNAL in April 1879 excitedly told their readers about the visit of the Prince and Princess of Wales to Hunstanton, describing how the eight miles from Sandringham to the town was garlanded with flowers, bunting and decorations.

CELEBRATION OF THE CORONATION [of George IV] July 28th 1821 — *At Saffron Walden, an ox was given by subscription to the public, but while in the process of roasting, news arrived that the Queen was prohibited from participating in the ceremony of the day — this operated on the feelings of a large party like an electric shock. In a moment, the carcase of the bullock was attacked, literally torn piecemeal off the spit and scattered in every direction.*

Sandringham House

At Bury St. Edmunds, much inconvenience was experienced during the illumination from a wanton practice of firing pistols close to passing females, and late at night several panes of glass were broken at the Angel Inn. Much of the evening's rumpus was down to Captain Bennet's Troup of Yeomanry and locals coming to blows, having drunk a good deal.

NORFOLK, YARMOUTH & LYNN COURIER

THE NORFOLK BROADS — *The Princess Louise has returned from a trip to the Norfolk Broads. That is conclusive; the halo of Royalty is now cast about them. The Norfolk Broads were first discovered by Mr. Charles Clowes of Norwich, about 7 years ago. It is true they had previously been visited in yachts and traversed by punters, but the idea of fitting out a trading wherry as a floating house, turning it for a time into a home, originated with Mr. Clowes.*

NORFOLK MAIL September 28th 1886

COTTON [on the occasion of Queen Victoria's Golden Jubilee] — *The Jubilee was celebrated here in such a manner as will not easily be forgotten. The proceedings began with a Thanksgiving service in the church, the prayers being read by the Rector (Rev. M. Turner). At three o'clock, the whole of the inhabitants sat down to a bountiful dinner provided in a spacious tent erected in a meadow by the Rector. After dinner, sports were commenced and kept up until 7 o'clock, when all sat down to a good tea. Sports were renewed afterwards, and kept up with great energy till nearly 10 o'clock, when a good display of fireworks took place, given and managed by Lieut. Brinkley. Miss Turner, who has been indefatigable in her exertions to make the proceedings successful, presented the prizes to the winners in the different sports.*

WEEKLY IPSWICH JOURNAL June 24th 1887

Traditionally, our local papers have been strongly supportive of the monarchy, whatever their shortcomings, as this item demonstrates.

NORWICH — *Monday last being the anniversary of the martyrdom of Charles I, the best of kings, hellishly butchered by the worst of villains, the same was religiously observed in this city.*

NORWICH GAZETTE February 4th 1727

16

Just for fun

WANTED — *A female who has a knowledge of fitting boots of a good moral character.*

LYNN NEWS March 8th 1873

COPIED FROM A TAX RETURN
One horse, I keep to draw a cart,
With wooden springs and apron smart,
A groom — occasional of course,
Who tells me news and cleans my horse.
One dog, I have, whose work is light;
He picks a bone and barks at night.
The impost on these things I'll pay,
For 'taxes are blessings' some folks say:
On me, the benefit is lost;
I have no pension but the cost.

SUFFOLK CHRONICLE June 8th 1822

The IPSWICH JOURNAL for March 20th 1824 included a lovely story about a popular practical joke of the time. Ipswich along with a lot of other towns employed nightwatchmen, popularly known as 'Charleys'. To protect them against the weather, sentry boxes were

erected at corners of the town. It was not unusual for these watch-
men to take a nap inside their sentry box. Drunken revellers took
delight in tipping over the box from behind, trapping the dozing
Charley inside. In this way, a drunken party who had just left the
Ipswich Arms Inn, Lower Brook Street were arrested for attacking
John Sore, the watchman of the parish of St. Stephens. This offence
was taken so seriously that the leading offender was imprisoned
for six months.

> **WORSE THAN A PIG'S FACE** — *A Russian lady possessed of two*
> *or three millions of money has offered her hand and fortune to any man*
> *who can look on her without terror. Her visage resembles a death's head*
> *with horrid fidelity. The attraction of her millions, it is said, induced some*
> *rash young men to adventure; but at the moment of removing the mask,*
> *the most intrepid are congealed with terror.*
>
> SUFFOLK CHRONICLE January 4th 1817

> **GREAT YARMOUTH** — *Notice is hereby given that very lately has*
> *been stolen or stray'd between THIS TOWN and BOTESDALE in Suffolk,*

a slender-made sable-coloured BITCH, about six and thirty years old of the true vulgarian breed and readily answers to the fashionable name of VIPER-TONGUE.

Whoever will be so generous to bring her to the most honourable MR. MAURICE FOUL-MOUTH, master of the Sea Hog & Bear vessel, at his house near the chapel in Great Yarmouth, shall be amply rewarded with three yards of old rope (enough to hang any dog) and a piece of tar-paulin.

N.B. no greater reward will be offered.

IPSWICH JOURNAL October 1767

John Glyde, the nineteenth century historian, writing in the EASTERN DAILY PRESS around 1900, under the title 'Norfolk Oddities', tells the tale of William H. Renny, a sailor from Lynn who was befriended by a Quaker Gentleman to whom 'he' confessed 'he' was really Anna Maria Real, a woman. Her lover left her to go to sea so she followed him, disguised as a sailor and worked out her passage to Russia undetected. Arriving, she received news that her sweetheart was dead, but liking a sailor's life, continued till she came back to Lynn eventually, and set up as a tailor, a trade learned aboard ship. Sometime after, a menagerie of wild beasts came to Norfolk, and the showman turned out to be none other than Maria Real's sweetheart. We are not told what happened after that.

Newspapers have always relied on their entertainment value. Here are just a few items published with fun in mind.

WASHED ASHORE – *On Monday morning, a bottle was washed ashore here containing a piece of paper on which was the following – 'Four p.m. Monday June 18th 1872. Longitude 10½ West, Latitude 52.7 North. Sinking (water gaining on us) The Golden Hind of and for London. Captain washed overboard. Fred Everett, first mate.' This is evi-*dently a hoax played by some stupid fellow. [All the more evident as the grid reference is in the middle of Germany!]

YARMOUTH & NORTH NORFOLK CONSTITUTIONALIST
September 7th 1872

At one of our commercial hotels, a stout red-faced gentleman in a white beaver blue coat and buff vest, offered to wager a sovereign that he would close his eyes and, simply by taste, name any kind of liquor in the house. The bet was taken and the process of winning or losing commenced forthwith.

'That is genuine brandy,' said the fat gentleman, tasting from a wineglass. 'And this is whiskey' . . . and so on. At length, a wag poured out a glass of water which he handed to the connoisseur. 'This is – ah – this is,' said he, tasting it with a grin. 'By thunder, gentlemen, I lose the bet! I never tasted this liquor before.'

YARMOUTH INDEPENDENT March 7th 1863

On Sunday night, a journeyman bricklayer near St. Giles Church who had a handsome wife met with the following adventure – coming home about eleven o'clock, a little in liquor, he found his wife in bed, but knocking hard at the door some time, she got up and let him in, when he immediately went to bed. In a few minutes, his wife complained most terribly of the cholic, and he being very good-natured, proposed getting up and fetching a dram from the next public house which he greatly approved of; but on recollection thought a pint of the Hot would do more good. The husband accordingly went for the hot and on paying for it, told the landlady to examine the three pence he had given her to see that the half-pence are good. She smiled and told him they were too good for her, being six guineas.

At this point he seems to have realised he had, in his hurry, put on a pair of trousers that were not his own; no wonder the wife was keen to send him on an errand.

The man stared and on examining his pocket found four more guineas and two half-guineas with a very handsome gold watch and that his breeches were changed into black velvet.

The account goes on to tell how he delayed confronting his wife but noticed how quickly she recovered from her cholic. In the morning

he shewed her the breeches and money and turned her down stairs with a particular desire that she should come to him no more. Then he got up and dressed himself and, instead of going to work, went to all his acquaintances to shew how valuable an exchange he had got for his wife.

NORWICH MERCURY May 15th 1756

TERRINGTON PETTY SESSIONS *— Jane Dixey of Emneth pleaded guilty to being drunk at Walsoken on 8th Feb. Defendant was seen by Sergeant Lockett so drunk that he had to send a man home with her.*

LYNN NEWS February 22nd 1873

And how about these dictionary definitions of words from the SUFFOLK CHRONICLE for 1824:

Celibacy — a vow by which the priesthood in some countries swear to content themselves with the wives of other people.

Flattery — Throwing dust in people's eyes, generally for the purpose of picking their pockets.

Hero — a wholesome butcher of men

Martyr — That which all faiths have produced in about equal proportions; so much easier is it to die for religion than to live for it.

Medicine — Guessing at nature's intentions and wishes, and then endeavouring to substitute our own.

Negro — A creature treated as a brute, because he is black, by greater brutes who happen to be white.

Ring — A circular link put through the snouts of swine and upon the finger of women, to hold them both in subjection.

Watering Places — Sundry, barren, shingly, chalky spots upon the coast, disfigured with frail lath and plaster bow-windowed tenements, which being supplied with scanty white dimity curtains, a few rickety chairs and tables, and some knotty featherless feather-beds, are considered to be furnished. Hither thousands resort during the six weeks of an English Summer, to ride in an impoverished species of wheelbarrow drawn by jaded donkeys or ponies, to sit on the pebbles and pelt them into the sea, to catch cold by walking on wet sands, to lose money in raffles, and enjoy at least one pleasant morning – that on which they return home.

In a SWAFFHAM JOURNAL story, a local curate was giving a sermon to his parishioners under the fatherly gaze of an elderly pastor, who afterwards complimented him on his sermon, but had certain reservations, pointing out that he used too many technical phrases for largely labouring community.

'Technical phrase; what can you mean?' asked the young man.
'You spoke of drawing inferences,' replied the old pastor. 'I'll wager even the cleverest of your flock would not understand you.'

They agreed to put it to the test, so a local farmer was waylaid and asked if he could draw an inference.

'Well, I suppose I could,' he replied, 'I've a team of horses that can draw anything to which they are hitched, but I don't think they should do it on a Sunday.'

SWAFFHAM JOURNAL March 1st 1879

The EASTERN DAILY PRESS (July 24th 1894) recounts the tale of an athlete named Sandow, author of a book entitled *Physical Training*, who had found it impossible to get work and was reduced to his last pennies in Amsterdam. According to the story, he hit upon a way to advertise his athleticism. He searched the city for all the weight-lifting slot-machines and, putting a penny into each, broke them all. He was arrested but claimed as he had paid the fee, he was entitled to try his strength. He was acquitted. He attracted so much attention, he was able to command fees of 1200 guilders a week.

A letter of thanks following an invitation to dinner
Tho' my dinner, dear Sir, was homely enough;
Part ragged, part raw, part rotten, part tough,
Tho' thy small single fish, well accustomed to shore
Had been out of water a fortnight or more,
Tho' thy lamb looked as green as the grass it had fed on,
And thy beef had the haut gout of a thing that is far gone,

Though thy patties occasioned the nauseous suggestion
Of meat that had passed the first stage of digestion,
Tho' thy steak had been cut from some canker-killed cow,
And the cook had scarce warmed the old lady through,
Tho' thy tarts had afforded a dainty repast
To the syrup cloyed blow-flies of the summer that's past;
Tho' thy windfalls called berries, the hogs would have slighted,
Tho' thy pickles were sweet and thy cheese, it was mited,
Yet I never enjoyed a more exquisite treat,
Thy wit made such ample amends for thy meat.

IPSWICH JOURNAL June 30th 1810

At the Cambridge Borough Sessions on Friday, a man named Robert
Lawler was sentenced to 6 months imprisonment for obtaining £10 from
Mrs. Owen upon presenting a palpably bad note, upon which were printed
the following words . . . The Royal Princess Bank No. 10,910. I promise
to perform to the public visiting this bank to the best of my ability every
evening or forfeit £10 or as many rounds of applause. By my own order
RIGDUM FUNNYBUS.

THETFORD & WATTON TIMES January 14th 1882

But, as has already been shown, much of the most amusing comment comes in the reporting of local stories, such as those with which we end this book.

EYE — *Late on Friday night . . . a daring robbery was committed on the*
premises of the Widow Moore in Church St. The thieves broke through
a wall and stole upwards of five stones of bacon. Suspicion fell upon a
'knight of the soot-bag' in whose crib about 6lbs of raw bacon was found
concealed in an old sheet. And on Monday, a well at the rear of the sweep's
house was dragged and lo! in a sack sunk by a heavy stone were fished
up 30lbs more of swine's flesh. His sable highness did not honour the
constables with his presence during the fishing ceremony, but it is likely
his 'Boston' majesty will soon take an airing on the highway to Ipswich,
previous to his long expected voyage across the herring-pond.

SUFFOLK CHRONICLE May 24th 1845

THE YARMOUTH WATER FROLIC

Our Frolic, last week, both on board and on shore,
Was the best frolic known since the days of old Noah
And shall be recorded, and therefore I chose
To describe it in verse, for it beggars all prose.
The morn treading lightly on Sonus's heel,
Was first ushered in by a monstrous good peal,
Then, the barges, but stop, only one barge was there
The rest were unluckily out of repair.
So the Mayor, (resolved that his friends should be merry)
Set on foot a subscription to fit out a wherry,
Where the whole Corporation with tables before 'em
Were stowed in the hold with the nicest decorum.
Then the wherries set sail and the Captain o'smack
His pop-guns discharged with a hell of a crack,
While on each side many thousand spectators
Hailed with loud accord these great navigators.
When arrived at their bounds, they made loud proclamation
And established the rights of this great corporation.

Yarmouth Water Frolic: painting by John and John Berney Crome

The business thus settled, the Mayor gave the word
To open the hampers and cover the board;
How they ripped up the pasties and scrambled for crust,
Dismembered the turkeys, the capons untrussed,
And unbuttoned their waistcoats for fear they should bust.

NORWICH MERCURY Summer 1777

Yes, I think we get the picture.

On Monday last, a fishing vessel belonging to Lowestoft, Robert Gowing, master, engaged in the mackerel fishery, was lying at sea about nine leagues to the Eastward of Lowestoft in 26 fathoms of water. The crew during the day cast their fishing lines into the sea for the purpose of catching cod-fish and haddock. Upon hauling up their lines, they had caught several cod . . . one was of unusual size, and the master proposed it should be brought on shore for sale, but being detained at sea until the following day it was agreed that the large cod-fish should be cleaned and dressed for the ensuing morning. Upon opening the fish, slitting its belly, a newborn infant, in a perfect state, presented itself to their almost unbelieving eyes. The master immediately summoned that part of the crew that were below, that the whole of them, nine in number, should witness this unprecedented phenomenon. They immediately began to examine the little innocent, which they describe as a very fine full-grown male child, perfectly formed with toe and fingernails complete, and having dark brown hair on the back part of its little head; and from its appearance it could not have been taken by the fish but a very few hours before it was caught.

SUFFOLK CHRONICLE June 1st 1833

Index